Star Quality

About the Author

Marjorie Orr has been a consultant astrologer for more than a decade and has an international reputation for her astrological writing in newspapers and magazines, and her broadcasts on radio and TV. She took an Honours Degree in Philosophy and English from Glasgow University and went on to a career in journalism and television production. While producing TV documentaries for the BBC in the 1970s, by chance she had her birth chart read, which sparked what became an all-consuming interest. She took up astrology as a full-time profession in the early 1980s and went on in addition to do a Jungian psychoanalytic training. Her Sun Sign columns in *Woman's Journal* and the *Daily* and *Sunday Express* are well known, as has been her writing on political and psychological astrology for the *Sunday Times*. Her work also appears in India, the Far East, Eire, the USA, Germany and Africa.

Star Quality

MARJORIE ORR

Aquarian/Thorsons
An Imprint of HarperCollins*Publishers*

The Aquarian Press
An Imprint of HarperCollins*Publishers*
77 – 85 Fulham Palace Road,
Hammersmith, London W6 8JB

Published by The Aquarian Press 1992
10 9 8 7 6 5 4 3 2 1

Marjorie Orr asserts the moral right to
be identified as the author of this work

A catalogue record for this book
is available from the British Library

ISBN 1 85538 179 6

Typeset by Harper Phototypesetters Limited,
Northampton, England
Printed in Great Britain by
HarperCollinsManufacturing Glasgow

CONTENTS

CHAPTER 1

CAN YOU SERIOUSLY BELIEVE IN THE STARS?

Why should sane, intelligent people take astrology seriously? The simplest answer is because it works. It provides information, in its own slightly peculiar fashion, that you cannot easily acquire elsewhere. That unpalatable truth strikes horror into the hearts of the rigidly rational. 'You can't possibly believe' they squeak 'in something you can't explain'. Why not? For hundreds of years no one knew why compasses worked, but if we had waited for explanations, much of the world would have been left unexplored.

'Suck it and see' is probably the best advice to give to anyone venturing into astrology. If it tells you something useful, use it. If it doesn't, try something else. The proof of the pudding is in the eating, but nowadays the problem is persuading people to try the first mouthful. The image of astrology is tainted by the fairground booth and gypsy earrings. It smells either of a con, or worse, of the black arts. The reality of modern psychological astrology, where many practitioners are university graduates, could not be more different.

A hard-headed television director friend of mine, having known me in my equally hard-headed pre-astrology days, was intrigued by my obvious interest in the subject, and decided to see whether an analysis of his birth chart would give him any useful pointers to his life. He saw one of the leading astrologers in London, who knew nothing about him.

His rather stunned comment afterwards was 'I had expected her to say a great cloud of things, from which I could select about ten per cent that would be right. But everything seemed to mean something – I found I couldn't put any of it aside. I was deeply impressed by the accuracy of it. It was a snapshot of my psyche and what was going on in my life.'

That kind of astonishment is common among those consulting astrology for the first time. The actor Anthony Hopkins, a Capricorn, had thought astrology at odds with astronomy and therefore of no interest, but found the proof in the predictions. I had made an astrological tape for him, unsolicited, as part of a television programme idea. He went filming for several months before he listened to it. 'My instant reaction was one of amazement . . . at how accurate it was. Now I don't think it is unscientific.'

Chay Blyth, the round-the-world yachtsman, never one to mince his words, wasn't very interested by the notion of astrology – he totally forgot our first appointment. Having finally arrived and heard a few of the home truths buried in his chart, he admitted with a grudging chuckle. 'On a scale of 1 to 10, my interest in this stuff before I met you was about 0–½. From what you've told me, it's now 6 or 7.' He is a down-to-earth Taurean, a very canny Scot, not given to wild flights of fancy.

Show business has always found it easiest to admit to an interest. Evangeline Adams, who died in 1932, had a star-packed clientele. Enrico Caruso, apparently, would not book tours until Adams had cleared the dates with the heavens. Tallulah Bankhead never made a career move without her. In addition to J.P. Morgan, Reginald Vanderbilt (Gloria's father) consulted her regularly before investing. Mae West was also a vocal fan of astrology, and used it to plan her career and make financial decisions. She died a multi-millionairess.

John Lennon often consulted astrologers, according to the US grapevine; as one might expect, Yoko Ono, with her Eastern background, is even more interested. She is reputed to use astrology and numerology to great effect in running her half-billion pound business empire.

The hardline scientists are appalled at the notion of astrology, because it undermines their entire view of how the universe is put together.

Scientific Evidence

In France, a country much smitten with the stars, a psychologist called Gauquelin set out to blow the whistle on what he regarded as an obvious nonsense. He fed the birth data of thousands of soldiers, doctors and artists into a computer to prove that the position of planets at their birth was irrelevant to their careers. What happened? He produced what is still the major scientific evidence that astrology does work, demonstrating that the position of planets at key points in the sky does 'produce' different psychological temperaments.

This did not please the scientific establishment. The much-publicized Committee for the Scientific Investigation of Claims of the Paranormal, which flaunts Nobel Prize winners amongst its members, set out to discredit his work. Their experiments threw up similar results to Gauquelin. What did they do in the name of scientific truth? They suppressed them! It took them five years to admit it, and only then because Gauquelin threatened to sue!

What lies behind much of their dislike of astrology, as part of the paranormal field, is fear. Arthur Koestler relates how he told his friend, the philosopher of science Hans Reichenbach, that certain ESP tests had been vetted accurate. The scientist turned pale. Koestler quotes him as saying 'If that is true it is terrible, terrible. It would mean I would have to scrap everything and start again from the beginning.'

Because it has this remarkable and yet unexplained ability to lay bare the workings of the psyche, the astrological birth chart is used in the UK, in the US and on the Continent, in counselling and psychotherapy. What it reveals about family background and parental influence, often sources of great confusion and unhappiness in people's lives, can be the saving of their sanity. Far from taking responsibility away from you, which is often the impression given, the self-knowledge astrology provides can increase the control you have over your affairs.

Sarah Lawson, a film producer and executive working in London for an American television network, was given an astrological consultation as a fun birthday present in Los Angeles. 'Suddenly you find a vast science there. I think people in Britain are embarrassed because it is unusual, and frightened because they think it eliminates freedom of choice. Once you make it clear that you're not using astrology to replace your initiative, it is enormously useful for putting one's life into context.'

Astrology also has its adherents in quite another sphere – the Stock Exchange, where the planetary movements are studied to see how they affect the rise and fall of currencies and investments.

Robert Hand, one of the leading American astrologers and a graduate in Philosophy of Science from Princeton, learned his craft early from his father, who dabbled in the markets using astrology. He never made a million, but acquired enough to indicate that there are more things in heaven and earth than we know. Packages of astrological systems are now on offer, in Britain and in the US, whose makers swear they can and do regularly predict market trends. There is also an astrological financial journal in the UK which claims to predict swings.

J.P. Morgan, the American financier, was a regular client of Evangeline Adams, the renowned New York astrologer in the early years of this century. He is quoted – how apocryphally I don't know – as saying 'Millionaires don't use astrology, billionaires do!'

Donald Regan's book on the Reagans specified the quite extraordinary figure of 48 per cent of Wall Street brokers using astrology in their business. Certainly in the past few years the *Wall Street Journal* has published well over thirty articles on the subject.

Recently when a joint US – Japanese stock market analyst group was set up, the Japanese insisted that astrology be included as a category of analysis. The Eastern culture, conditioning, and educational systems are much better balanced than they are in the West, giving due weight to both right brain and left brain attitudes. The Japanese admit to the value of the admittedly irrational but nonetheless vital input of subjects like astrology.

In Britain the leading financial astrologer, Daniel Pallant, started life as a trader on the Metals Markets. He was perplexed by the fluctuations in prices and started a massive breakdown on his computer of the FT Index through its history to try to pin down the cycles. He now has over twenty of the largest investment trusts and unit trust companies as his clients, plus many private investors.

He accurately forecast the timing, though not the

scale, of the 1987 Stock Market crash. A German astrologer, Wolf Angermeyer, did foresee the extent of the impending crunch. An ex-Managing Director, who in his retirement is now a full-time predictor, he told a conference a few months earlier to be out of the markets by late summer. The crash happened in October.

Every astrologer uses different techniques. Pallant uses a complex breakdown of the Stock Index for his assessments. Working on a much simpler base using the United Kingdom chart, I forecast a period of major financial trauma starting in late autumn 1987 running to the early 1990s. Both methods, remarkably, arrive at the same conclusions.

Path to the Stars

The newer breed of astrologer is often a graduate, probably in psychology or philosophy, and most of them study for further diplomas for counselling. In 1985, London University awarded a Ph.D. – to psychologist Michael Startup – for statistical investigations into astrology.

My own interest in astrology, though quite unexpected, stemmed from my fascination with epistemology, studied as part of a Philosophy degree at Glasgow. Epistemology means theory of knowledge – how we know things. Astrology was one information source nobody taught me about at university.

While I was producing a BBC documentary series on the paranormal, in the 1970s, an astrologer volunteered to read my chart. Until then, I doubt if I could have told you what my sun sign was, and had certainly never read a horoscope column. I was astonished at what he told me about my past. He could identify the patterns of my life and behaviour from knowing only the time, date and place of my birth.

I left flabbergasted and headed straight for a book

shop. Astrology, unlike crystal ball gazing, did seem to be learnable from the written word. Julia and Derek Parker's *Compleat Astrologer* gave me the groundwork and basic calculations.

Other writers, like Liz Greene, Robert Hand, Stephen Arroyo and Howard Sasportas, gave me depth and interpretation. I practised on my friends. My enthusiasm, notoriously flighty normally, held up as the evidence continued to roll in. It actually seemed to work, and what's more, you didn't need to be a clairvoyant to master it.

A retentive mind helps, especially one that likes jig-saw puzzles, piecing together a huge number of variables. At an advanced level, like many professions, it becomes more of a synthesizing talent than just-follow-the-instructions-on-the-card. It is a little like medical diagnosis or cookery: the ground rules are the same but, depending on the practitioner, the results can differ slightly.

The scientific proofs are all-important for the intelligentsia, and, it must be said, for men, who appear to be less open-minded, if not actually afraid, about what appears to them to be irrational. Women, perhaps more in tune with monthly cycles, are instinctively aware at least of the lunar effect, and historically less involved in the creation of today's philosophy with its emphasis on a mechanical world view.

It is now known, for instance, that the moon affects not only the tides and behaviour patterns of shellfish such as oysters, but also the rate of bleeding of surgical patients. In Russia surgeons make a point, where possible, of avoiding the full moon for operations. Radio transmissions are affected by the relative positions of planets. There is more interference when planets are at angles traditionally regarded by astrologers as difficult.

There were major earthquakes on America's west coast early in the 1980s, at a time predicted by astrologers. The close proximity of the planets Jupiter and Saturn was the trigger. Jupiter represents expansion and Saturn contraction, so the combination was explosive. Interestingly, astronomers now have a theory that it was the combined light of those two planets, when very close together, which created the bright star that led the wise men to the stable where Jesus was born.

Sunny Side Up

Although astrology's image is improving, many still have reservations about the daily, weekly and monthly columns in newspapers and magazines. Sun sign astrology, as the simple variety is known, is based on the position of the sun at birth. It offends some of the old-style traditional practitioners of the starry arts almost as much as it offends the rationalists. The purist astrologer sunk in the intricacies of the Uranus quincunx, your Aquarian ascendant in T square to Mars and Pluto, and other such astrological niceties, feels demeaned by the simplicity of it all.

To be sure, the regular columns at the light end of the market compare with serious personal charts in the same way that Barry Manilow compares with Beethoven. However, you can listen to and enjoy both. Many of today's practising astrologers were enticed into studying further through reading a particularly accurate magazine prediction. Market research surveys for newspapers show the astrology columns to be amazingly popular. Out of twenty-five regular features in newspapers, they come within the top five – often in the first two.

Naturally enough, anything as simplified as sun sign astrology is going to be less specific, less accurate than the serious variety. But the predictions and personality analysis are amazingly sound, given the limitations.

Historical Roots

For the intellectually superior who still remain sceptical, a quick skip through astrology's long, substantial and illustrious history may help. Much of the present-day astrology is rooted in the writings of Ptolemy, circa 70 AD, though we know it was used several thousand years ago. The Arabs developed mathematics around the eighth century to improve their astrology, and handed it on to Europe via the Crusaders. At one time in the Middle Ages no king, court or Holy Roman Emperor was without a resident astrologer. The subject was even taught in the church colleges and universities.

All the early astronomers were also astrologers – Galileo, Kepler, Bacon. Even Sir Isaac Newton, he of the apple and theory of gravity, was an unwilling believer – unwilling because he couldn't explain its accuracy. William Lilly, the famous seventeenth-century astrologer, whose mammoth definitive *Christian Astrology* has now been reprinted, played an intriguing role in the political life of the country. He managed to advise both Oliver Cromwell and Charles I at the same time when they were on opposite sides in the Civil War. Quite neat work, that – and he kept his head intact.

It's not exactly clear why astrology fell into such disrepute in the West during the eighteenth and nineteenth centuries. The rise of Calvinism, capitalism and rationalism threw Europe and the US into an industrial revolution, squashing the expression of more mystical and intuitive qualities. In the East, however, astrology continued to be part of daily living, and it is still automatically assumed that a leader consults his astrologer along with other advisers. It would be the

15

height of irresponsibility not to test all advice available. Sheik Yamani had his astrologer, and Indira Gandhi certainly used hers regularly.

The timing of events in the East is often left to astrologers. A classic example is the Independence of Burma in 1948, which was set to coincide with Jupiter rising in favourable aspect to Moon and Venus. The fact that well before dawn – 4.20 am local time – was hardly convenient was disregarded. The annual Independence Day Parade is still held every year at the same time (though given the history of Burma since 1948, one might query whether the astrologers got it quite right!)

Western leaders have to be more circumspect, although the available evidence suggests the current leaders of several countries are not above a quick dabble. President Roosevelt had fewer inhibitions – he used to keep his birth chart on the wall of his office as a reminder of his tendency to fly off the handle.

Ronald Reagan was always less honest. American astrologers had known for years that Reagan used astrology, despite his repeated denials, which was why his office issued no less than seven different birth times to confuse those outside who were trying to predict his future prospects. Without Donald Regan's intervention we might never have known for sure. From early on in his career Reagan used astrology to stage-manage important events, such as his first Inauguration as Governor of California. After midnight was judged the propitious moment and at that unlikely time, it all happened. Bush was also reckoned ideal as a running mate for Aquarian Reagan because he was Gemini, another air sign.

Why the Reagans and the great American public should have been so wary of the use of astrological advice is not remotely clear. Past adherents of astrology include not only Teddy Roosevelt, but further back Benjamin Franklin and Thomas Jefferson. Those two great founding fathers were both ardent proponents of the subject. They insisted that the Declaration of Independence be ratified by July 4 1776 because they knew that the combination of the planets on that day were excellent for the long-term establishment of a peaceful and prosperous country.

President J.F. Kennedy's father is known to have consulted London astrologers during his ambassadorship in London; even General George Patton is reckoned to have used it in military manoeuvres.

Slowly, astrology is regaining credibility in the West, although businessmen, politicians and others in public or influential positions who regularly use its information can still be remarkably shy about broadcasting the fact. One prominent businessman and politician, who will admit in private his interest, often invites astrologers to his parties. 'You would be surprised' he told me once, 'how many of my friends and colleagues creep back under the cover of darkness to consult them.' But few will stand up and admit to it . . . yet.

CHAPTER 2

ASTROLOGY –
A TREASURE TRAIL

The real excitement of astrology is that it actually works. Common sense says that every twelfth person cannot possibly be similar. And yet, and yet. You look at friends and workmates and the Geminis do fidget and chatter, the Aries compete like mad, Scorpios plot and plan, Pisces daydream, and the Taureans stand firm no matter what.

Occasionally you do meet people who don't fit the pattern. They aren't the exceptions that prove the rule. They are, sadly, just plain out of touch with their centre. If they could reconnect they would blossom.

Accentuate the Positive

Do you read the pluses and minuses of your star sign, nod sagely as your virtues and talents are unfolded, wince at the black marks, and then just sit back? Why not take a full-frontal view of what you are good at? By harnessing your own particular talents, you could be taking a huge step to greater contentment in the future. Why stay a square peg in a round hole?

Most people feel failures because they aren't doing what they are good at. If you are a dreamy, sympathetic, creative Pisces, why give yourself ulcers because you aren't a precise, clear cut, thinking Virgo? Go Pisces, where your vision, your compassion, and your intuition will be of most use.

Geminis, stop beating yourself about the head because you can't concentrate on one subject for more than ten minutes at a time. You have rare talent for knowing a tiny bit about a million different things. Never mind the lack of depth, feel the width! Aries don't have Libra's tact and ability to relate, but they have qualities that Libra totally lacks like decisiveness, courage and leadership ability.

Relocate the Negative

Do you live with self-loathing and resigned apathy about your less-than-wonderful traits? Try a bit of lateral thinking and see where those traits have a positive function. Take Aries, who can be brutally insensitive to the feelings of others and bad at relationships, always 'me first'. Where is that a positive virtue? In leaders, for one thing, who have to stand alone and rely on their own judgement. OK, so they have to be open to feedback, but when it comes to the crunch, leaders need total confidence in themselves. Aries have it.

Taurus, in a different way, will hold their ground no matter what. Their fault is a terrible stubbornness, but in the right place that oak-tree immovability can be a godsend. So if your life, Taurus, is an endless series of hassles with others screaming at you to compromise, don't try to turn yourself into an ever-flexible birch tree. Someone, somewhere needs that wonderful, placid, rooted, earthy temperament.

Virgos moan and nitpick like mad, but in the right setting that perfectionist, analytical streak will bring order to the most confused situations. Leos demand attention and an audience, sometimes in a highly tiresome fashion. But where would we be without entertainers and bosses?

Libras dither over decisions and always need a second opinion, but that thoughtful deliberation which won't leap at the instant answer and takes everyone's views into consideration is just the thing for lawyers, diplomats and those who work with the public.

Scorpios play their cards so close to their chest you know they have to be up to no good. Yet if you are ever in need of a discreet ear for a confidence, no one is better.

Cancer can't let go. The pain of separation makes them hang on beyond the bounds of common sense. But all that emotional hyper-sensitivity tunes them into other people's needs quite amazingly.

Sagittarius has a brutal honesty, but if you want a straight answer that is exactly what you are looking for. Capricorn often can't play happily. They feel they ought to be up and doing all the time. But their strength is precisely that: frivolities won't distract them – so they are achievers and organizers *par excellence*.

Life is a See-Saw

Every energy has a plus and a minus way of working. It isn't always instantly clear how to turn your energies round, and see where your faults can be used as positive virtues. For most of us it is the major task of adult life, but the rewards are well worth the effort.

Let's face it, at the end of the day, even if you are in absolutely the right niche and the right relationships, you won't be all perfect. The shadow side is always there, and ultimately just has to be accepted. But there is a world of difference in living out what you are as fully as you can, light and shade, and trying to submerge bits of the essential you because circumstances or other people seem to require it.

Where Lies the Guilt

So your mother-in-law can't stand you and you never quite matched up to daddy's specifications? Why does it have to be your fault? Your mother-in-law's Scorpio and you are an Aquarian. Two very stubborn signs – a clash was inevitable. It may very well suit her to tell you it's your fault. Scorpios are excellent Machiavellian strategists; in-fighting is their speciality. She has probably beaten down the rest of the opposition in the family long ago, but it isn't actually a weakness in your character that you stick to your views, unwilling to be hauled into her brooding emotional depths. You just happen to be different, and the chemistry doesn't work. *Avoid her*.

Daddy is a Sagittarian and wanted you to be a teacher, highly principled, pony-mad as a child, and fired with his enthusiasms. You loathe the big, muddy outdoors, children and conventional morals in equal quantities. Computers are what rouse you to excitement, plus deeply avant-garde discussion about the sexual revolution. So what? He's a Sagittarian – tell him to live out his own life and you'll live out yours. In an Aquarian way.

Be Yourself

That is what astrology is really about: helping you find out who you are, and helping you maximize your potential. But before you do that you need to find your centre: the core of talents, feelings and drives which makes you who you can be. That isn't easy, especially since most parents seem quite incapable of letting children develop in their own individual right.

Try to mould a child like a lump of plasticine and you may well succeed with the outer personality shell, but the cost will be high. There will be a very damaged, angry, outraged, hurt little individual hiding inside that

21

shell, who doesn't really know who they are. And that is where the astrology comes in.

It is the map which will lead you to the buried treasure at the centre of the maze – the individual human being. Since no one has parents who don't try in some ways to guide their footsteps, no one starts adult life knowing themselves inside out. We are all trying to find the missing links.

Elementary Hints

The twelve signs are divided into four elements. Fire – Aries, Leo, Sagittarius; Earth – Taurus, Virgo, Capricorn; Air – Gemini, Libra, Aquarius; Water – Cancer, Scorpio, Pisces. Each element has its own special resonance. Fire is enthusiastic, imaginative, earth is practical and well-organized, air is mental and water emotional.

An emotional watery child will have a hard time in a home with very airy parents. Cancer and Pisces especially are desperately sensitive. Surrounded by very laid back, detached, mental types who never seem to care about anything, Cancer will reverse back under its shell and sulk endlessly, Pisces will disappear off into fantasies and daydreams. They can't live out what they are, and what they feel, in what for them is an arid atmosphere.

In the reverse situation, airy children will run a mile from a watery atmosphere. All that soggy, under-mining, unstable emotion. They feel in serious danger of being drowned. Give them space.

Fire children, and adults, for that matter, need to let their enthusiasms rip. Surrounded by too much earth – all organization and common sense – they feel life has lost its spark and its meaning.

Earthy personalities, on the other hand, view fiery people with horror. Give Capricorn, who views life as a most serious business, a restless Aries or a wildly impractical Sagittarius to bring up and there is bound to be conflict – unless Capricorn is very evolved, or put it another way, if Capricorn is fully him- or herself.

Only undeveloped, insecure temperaments need to turn their children, friends, adult family or workmates into what they want them to be. If you have found your centre and are living it out, you will be quite happy to be you, and equally happy to let everyone else be themselves.

Not only are you unhappy if you are an underactive Aries, an over-conventional Aquarius, totally compromised Scorpio, or meek Leo – everyone in your surrounding environment catches it too. Your unlived bits find other channels and attach themselves to other people. Quite unconsciously, you try to turn others into what you should be but aren't. In so far as you aren't living out your own life, you are dumping that burden on to those around you, particularly children, and often your loved ones.

Develop Your Potential
Binoculars don't help. If it isn't visible, you need techniques to help you, to get underground and lead you to where your buried potential is waiting to be discovered. Most people don't live out distorted versions of themselves by choice: they just don't know who they are. If they did, they would off and *be* it.

Astrology is the map which will help guide you on the great mystery tour through the enchanted forest to find the treasure chest, or the Grail, or whatever metaphor you like to put on your own personal meaning.

It won't walk the path for you. Knowing in your head what you are doesn't magically turn you into it, but at least you'll know the right direction to look. As the old

23

adage says 'If you look where you are going, you'll go where you are looking.'

Specialist astrologers tend to sneer at newspaper and magazine astrology which focuses on sun signs, i.e. the birthday sign. However, even if you have a personal horoscope drawn up, the absolute core of your identity will be indicated by your sun sign, which shows where the sun was at the time you were born. Your personal chart will add all sorts of subtleties and nuances of character interpretation via the positions of the other nine planets in our solar system at the moment of your birth. But the central issue of your individuality hinges on that single sun sign, whatever it may be.

Serious Astrology

The personal birth chart is simply a map of the heavens at the exact moment of birth as seen from the place where you were born. Imagine yourself as you pop out into the world at 00.00 hours of your life. Had you been able to look upwards with super stellar vision, you would have seen the relative positions of the planets as they travel through the solar system. There is the Sun, the Moon, and eight planets – Mercury, Venus, Mars, Jupiter, Saturn, Uranus, Neptune and Pluto.

Astrology uses their positions in the different signs – e.g. Moon in Virgo and Venus in Taurus – to define certain characteristics about a personality. Don't ask why: most of the information came down from antiquity and it just appears to work. Moon in Virgo people do worry themselves out of sight.

Serious astrology pins much on the accurate birth time, because that tells what was on the horizon when a person is born. This sign, known as the Ascendant sign, indicates the face you show the world and is almost as important as the sun sign.

As if that wasn't enough, calculations are made

which show what angles planets stood at one to another. If Saturn is square Neptune at ninety degrees that indicates an unclear relationship between the person's sense of reality and their sense of fantasy. Often it produces a slightly paranoid personality.

Once the horizon has been fixed, the personal birth chart is then completed by dividing the circular map of the heavens into twelve segments called houses. Each of them carries a different significance. Again, there seems to be no reasons why that makes sense. But if you are born with the Sun at the centre of the heavens then you do appear to be hard-driving and successful; if born with the Sun at the lowest point, you are home-loving and family oriented.

Astrology is extremely pragmatic, and astonishingly accurate. Forget about the explanations of why, just look at the evidence.

Star Signs
(NB: These are approximate, because the start and finish dates of the signs can shift by one or two days in different years. Those on the cusp should consult an astrologer.)

Aries	March 21–April 20
Taurus	April 21–May 20
Gemini	May 21–June 21
Cancer	June 22–July 23
Leo	July 24–August 23
Virgo	August 24–September 23
Libra	September 24–October 22
Scorpio	October 23–November 22
Sagittarius	November 23–December 22
Capricorn	December 23–January 20
Aquarius	January 21–February 19
Pisces	February 20–March 20

CHAPTER 3

ARIES STARS

IN A NUTSHELL
Hotheads, politicians, winners and incredibly tough women.

Film

Marlon Brando, Sir Alec Guinness, Eddie Murphy, Sir John Gielgud, Peter Ustinov, Charlie Chaplin, Rod Steiger, Joan Crawford, Debbie Reynolds, Carol White, Gloria Swanson, Ali McGraw, Julie Christie, Doris Day, Mary Pickford, Dirk Bogarde, Paul Michael Glaser, Gregory Peck, Anthony Perkins, Richard Chamberlain, Warren Beatty, Omar Sharif, James Caan, Hayley Mills, Bette Davis.

Film Directors

Cubby Broccoli, Francis Ford Coppola, Akira Kurosawa, Nagisa Oshima, David Lean, Lindsay Anderson.

Music

Elton John, Andrew Lloyd Webber, Stephen Sondheim, Eric Clapton, David Cassidy, Alan Price, Howard Keel, James Last, Diana Ross, Paul Robeson, Pearl Bailey, Billie Holliday, Aretha Franklin, Chaka Khan, Merle Haggard, Emmylou Harris, André Previn, Hammer.

Sport
Sevvy Ballesteros, Vincent O'Brien, Clare Francis, Paul Schockemohle, Bobby Moore, Gabriela Sabatini, Jonjo O'Neill, Jack Brabham, Sue Barker.

Writers
Arthur Hailey, Jeffrey Archer, Tom Sharpe, Kingsley Amis, Leslie Thomas, John Fowles, George MacDonald Fraser, Edgar Wallace, Paul Theroux, Alan Ayckbourn, Catherine Gaskin, Gloria Steinem.

Art
Goya, Leonardo da Vinci, Vincent van Gogh, J.S. Bach, Rachmaninov, Wordsworth, Swinburne, Baudelaire, Robert Frost.

Lovers
Hugh Hefner, Casanova.

Thinkers
Descartes, Hobbes, A.J.P. Taylor, Joseph Pulitzer.

The ranks of the rich and the famous Aries are awash with unashamed winners – not surprising for a sign which puts top priority on being *numero uno*. Andrew Lloyd Webber, with a string of musical successes; Marlon Brando, who commands a huge movie star fee; Jeffrey Archer with his spate of hugely bestselling novels; David Frost, in his day *the* name in TV on both sides of the Atlantic: not always hugely well liked, but always there at the finish, preferably first past the post. Other Aries include Vincent O'Brien, probably the most outstanding race horse trainer ever, certainly the richest. Joseph Pulitzer, by giving his name to the American literary prize, is guaranteed a permanent place up with the winners.

Bestselling novelists figure prominently. George MacDonald Fraser, Leslie Thomas, Edgar Wallace, John Fowles. Not always desperately subtle, but strong on imagination and popular appeal. Aries, being a fire sign, is fuelled by fantasy, tales of derring-do, and great courage. It adores heroism.

Renowned lovers, from Casanova to Warren Beatty and Hugh Hefner, exhibit another Aries trait. They are great romantics, but stronger on quantity than staying power. They adore the chase, the struggle, the victory, another notch on the bed-post. But stay put? That's when the tedium sets in.

Aries is ruled by Mars, a very masculine fighting energy, which is possibly why most of the renowned Aries women have an abrasive edge. Strong men must have quailed before Joan Crawford, Bette Davis *et al*.

A survey of British MPs showed Aries to be one of the two most common signs in Parliament. Obvious, since winning the seat is a *sine qua non* for the job. It is probably also a major contributing factor to the noise levels at prime minister's question time. Aries is fiery, hot-headed and, with maturity, strong on leadership qualities.

Aries in Essence
Action is Aries' primary mode of reaction. Some signs think, some feel deeply, others plan. Aries' instantaneous response is to leap up and do almost anything, never mind the consequences. They may sometimes be a little short on sense, but short on courage – never. Self-confidence also comes in abundant supply, along with initiative, leadership ability, self reliance, intuition and inventiveness.

As the first sign of the zodiac, the sign of spring and new life bursting forth, Aries is often referred to as the baby of the star signs. It is a fairly warlike baby, to be sure, since Aries is ruled by Mars. The volume and the egocentricity can, in less evolved Aries, be extremely childish. Babies will throw a tantrum to catch your attention, no matter how inconvenient the moment. What they want, they want instantly. Patience is a virtue only learned late in life, if ever, by most Aries. They also have a baby's refreshing sense of being the most important person in the world. No false modesty, or delicate anguish about the feelings or rights of others. Number One is organized first, the rest can follow. Definitely, Me First.

Aries are straightforward to a fault, can be brash, have been known to be insensitive, but what a relief to have around when you need a strong opinion on the spot. On the whole they have no side, no devious strategy, and certainly won't please you by telling you what they think you want to hear. They don't care.

Relationships are not usually a strong point early in life. In order to relate, you do need to consider the other even just a tiny bit. This is not to say they don't have a strong sex drive; they can also be highly romantic. Candlelit dinners and black suspender belts set them aflame, but they much prefer brief flaring passions than anything too routine.

Aries may not have the stomach or the endurance to run marathons in life: the sixty-yard dash is more their style, but they certainly do not lack energy. And they know instinctively that the best way forward is straight through or over any obstacle which stands in their way. Full frontal confrontations, the prospect of which sends Pisces into a decline, are part of Aries' everyday routine. Face up to the problem, knock it down if necessary, and proceed on life's merry way.

You don't win by courting popularity, by being nice to people; you win by beating people, over the head if required. That's Aries' view of life's major lesson. And

29

don't doubt it works.

Diplomacy and tact are added as a veneer once Aries learns, as their vital juices dry up slightly, that you can win more easily, more quickly and therefore more often with a modicum of charm. But don't be fooled. The iron fist is never totally relaxed.

Fire signs, of which Aries is first and most assertive, Leo the middle and fixed, and Sagittarius last and most adaptable, are all highly intuitive. Not logical, not mental, just blessed with a strong imagination, great fantasizing ability, and an almost magical insight into solutions, plus a wonderfully spontaneous sense of humour.

Fiery people live up in the clouds, not down in boring reality on earth, and certainly not in their bodies. Practical Aries are not, grounded and organized they certainly are not, and you can never claim they are really in tune with their bodies. So eating, resting, exercising in rhythm with their body's needs is tricky for them. They either over- or underdo any combination, but it is often too little food, too much exercise and certainly not enough sleep.

Amongst men, quite often Aries produces eternal Peter Pans, young, mischievous, forever playing at life, looking for mothers and glamorous mistresses far into middle age. Maturity is not a favoured goal. With women the struggle is usually to find a balance between their femininity and their aggression.

Positive Traits
Original, inventive, assertive, competitive, full of initiative, intuitive, explorers, self-reliant, bulging with leadership ability, spontaneous, unself-conscious, very sexy, deeply romantic, extremely passionate, dashing, courageous, sporty, independent, direct, never admit defeat.

Negative Traits

Sulk if they don't win, arrogant, conceited, self-pitying, insensitive, have delusions of persecution, lack tact and diplomacy, lack staying power, self-centred, narrow, overbearing, brutal, thoughtless, impersonal, immodest, brash, aggressive, and never stop to consider the consequences.

Aries' Winning Streak

That continually restless, up-there-and-at-them energy of Aries, which never, never admits defeat, is what wins in the end. Success, being one part inspiration to nine parts determination, is just Aries' forte. All that fertile imagination produces ideas, and if the first fifteen ideas end up face down in a puddle – no matter. That resilient rubber ball quality just bounces back . . . with another fifteen.

Look closely at the famous Aries. Many of them have had terrible crashing defeats that would paralyse more sensitive souls for a lifetime. But 'Never Say Die' is Aries' main motto in life.

All that unself-conscious spontaneity that takes no heed of others produces highly original individuals – so don't try to be one of the herd. Make a virtue of being one of a kind. It's not only leaders who need to stand alone: so do explorers and pioneers. Elton John is an original in his work, so is Marlon Brando. There had never been anything like either of them before. Their courage paid off.

Aries as Lovers

At first sight nothing is more attractive, dashing, romantic. Aries won't mope about wondering whether you will reject their advances – whatever sex they are, they do the advancing. What they want, they want. And right now. It can be highly flattering.

Aries adore romance, the glamour of the seduction, the excitement of the chase – the ambience is all. Candlelit dinners, sexy underwear, wreathed in fantasy. But the problem comes once fantasy fades and real life begins, because Aries are short on staying power, and they loathe routine, mundane everyday life. And even the most passionate affairs have their down-to-earth moments.

Aries don't like the more tedious physical aspects of reality. Dandruff and ingrowing toenails seriously interfere with their chivalrous romances. Knights on white chargers don't think about things like that. Aries need to keep up the mystique. When that fades, they often fade with it.

As long as your wishes are not too earthy, Aries are wonderful lovers. But they like the fantasy, the atmosphere, the mood to be just right. Broad daylight, unglamorous surroundings, and a pre-clinch chat about the aftereffects of last night's curry put them into instant reverse gear.

Aries Get On With

Anyone who can put up with their shockingly direct opinions, their restless energy, and will let them win (after a respectable battle, of course). They adore the other fire signs Leo and Sagittarius, who share their joy of living, though Leo can grab too much of the attention at times. Water signs worry them. Pisces make Aries ill. They can't understand all that Pisces chaos, and inability to cope. Scorpio is far too heavy and won't fight clean.

Aries quite likes the earth signs because they can help to ground some of their more outrageous ideas and show them a practical way. Aries appreciates Capricorn's ability to get things done, though thinks they are fearfully over-serious. Aries admires Virgo's helpful common sense, though can't understand their reticence. Taurus they find a touch stubborn, and irritatingly placid.

The Air signs, on the whole, Aries thinks are too chilly. Sure, they have ideas, but they do not have enthusiasms. Gemini would be their choice of the air signs. Libra quite passes their comprehension except as a pet to follow at heel. They won't do what Aries loves above all else – have a good fight.

Aries as Children
Highly impatient! They tend to stay babies until the age of about thirty-six, but at least you should only have the first half of that to worry about as parents. And they do need life to knock them about a bit, so make them leave home as soon as possible.

Constant activity is a must. Don't worry if fiery junior finishes nothing s/he starts. Just keep the conveyor belt of projects running. Initiative at starting is their strength; endurance and adaptability their weakness. So put them where their talents can flourish. If your Aries mini is meek, unassertive, highly considerate, and indecisive, something is wrong. You have pushed them into their opposite – which is Libra. Their true nature needs to be retrieved.

Aries as Wives
On romantic, social, holiday sprees tremendous fun, the life and soul of private and public parties, and will make you the envy of other men. So if you have a constantly stimulating, exciting, social life with frequent trips thrown in, life all around will be A1. The bits in between may be more problematic. Aries ladies are not as a rule over-domestic, hate routine in any form, loathe the idea of being submissive little women. Independence is a major issue for them. They need a partnership of equals – at least!

Aries as Husbands

Same as above. They do adore flirting, so if you are jealous by nature, avoid Aries as husbands. Sometimes they do more than flirt. Older Aries men have much to offer, but they need a few hard knocks from life to teach them consideration, so eye younger ones with caution. Early in adult life, Aries men can be cruel.

They will not knock up shelves, mend blocked sinks, or help with the hoovering. But with luck, they'll be successful enough to pay for a home help and handymen. And they will also whirl you away on more romantic ventures, and make you forget the daily chores. If you want a dull, safe husband, don't pick an Aries. If you do get an Aries, I promise you won't ever be bored.

Aries as Bosses

Autocratic. Self-centred. Quite impossible at times. But don't be scared: they love a courageous opponent and a good punch up, and they do fight clean. It may be a bit brutal at times but it won't be underhand. Like husbands, you can expect Aries bosses to provide excitement rather than stability. They will not do the routine tasks – underlings are there to keep the organization and paperwork in order!

Aries as Slaves

Bad news. Could not be less well-designed. All that instant obedience, 'only thy will, not mine' – the thought of it gives Aries hypertension. Submission is only possible for so long, then the pressure cooker of Aries temper will blow – very loudly.

Favourite Saying

'I want it now!' Stamp. 'Why can't I have it now?' Crash.

Aries and Money

Not essentially practical, and terribly inclined to huge extravagances. The combination is often a recipe for disaster early on in adult life. Happily most Aries, though they aren't materialistic, do want success. With it comes money to pay for advisers and more glamorous goodies.

Aries up to the Millennium

The tremendous upheaval in your career and life's direction which created such havoc in the late 1980s is a continuing thread of uncertainty to 1995. By 1994 it has become obvious that an old way of life must end. Bitterness and hostility in intimate relationships ease considerably, as do career crises, in 1995. A difficult ten years of arguing about joint finances ends as well. You are now able to design a whole new philosophy of living for yourself. Saturn moving into Aries between 1996 and 1997 heralds a whole new identity for you and a new way of living. The eclipses in 1996 mark this out as your real turning point for the decade. The next four years are a steady progress through a forward-looking period where you are redesigning almost every area of your life. 1999 will be your year.

Diana Ross
26 March 1944

With Scorpio rising, Diana Ross can exude a strong sultry, secretive image and this, coupled with a fiery fifth house Sun, means she has the perfect flair for a high-profile show business career. She adores being in the spotlight, being the life and soul of the party. But behind this entertaining, highly feminine façade is a purposeful businesswoman who has known the harder side of life and grown a very thick skin.

She has successfully lost that Aries great start/bad

finisher streak because of a tough Saturn Mars contact. She knows how to slog on long after her interest has flagged, because she wants security in life and control over her finances, and above all because she had a childhood in which not much attention was paid to her wishes. So she can put aside her need for frivolity and indulgence just to put work first – a must for a successful show business career. However, with a fifth house Sun, her very genuine love of children must at times have created obstacles in the way of her ambitions.

Her chart is a wonderful combination of restless ambition, which keeps her constantly on the move, and dogged determination which must make her a formidable opponent in an argument – especially an emotional one. A solid Taurus Moon makes her aware of her sensations. She is keen always to dress in opulent fabrics, to surround herself with luxuries that taste good, smell good and look indulgent. What she wants she heads straight for at home. She can be enormously jealous of loved ones if her security feels threatened.

Curiously, her health is a little insecure, being much affected by the state of her emotions. So one day she feels up, the next day down. A strongly aspected Neptune also makes her worry too much, mainly about things which may never happen. She occasionally worries about people being against her, and barricades herself away.

An almost totally right-hand chart indicates a personality who is far from being independent. She needs the support of those around her at home in the family, children and loved ones, though her relationships will always be a little erratic.

Her career is in a lowish profile phase until 1995, when she starts on a new phase. Then it is onwards and upwards for another long span of success.

Dudley Moore
19 April 1935

The diminutive, quite unlikely Hollywood sex symbol shows another Aries trait – the eternal Peter Pan. Mischievous, full of fun, restless, devil-may-care. Never quite grown up, never quite settled down.

Uranus falls close to his Sun, which has perfectly fitted him for a business where unpredictability is the order of the day. There is always variety, travel, constant movement, constant buzz. Most people would find the perpetual restlessness of his life too tiring, but he thrives on high adrenalin flow.

Like many of the highly creative personalities born in the mid to late 1930s, he carries the Saturn Neptune opposition in his chart. At one level it gives him almost endless access to his creative unconscious, allowing him to live out his fantasies in his work. At another level, it makes him supersensitive to atmosphere and people.

He was born near the time of the Full Moon in Scorpio, so he is able to relate to people dramatically different in temperament from himself. He is also able to sacrifice himself and his needs for worthwhile objectives, and can be single-minded in his aims.

A lovely aspect in his chart between Jupiter in Scorpio, which is lucky with money, and Pluto gives him a superbly useful ability to turn thoughts into things. If he thinks something, often he can make it happen.

He thrives on an active social life, with Venus in Gemini, and is a witty, entertaining party guest. He keeps others entranced for hours with his sharp jokes, puns and word plays, and could write well if he chose to channel his talents onto paper. Underneath the colourful, friendly exterior he is shyer than he appears.

With Mercury also in Aries he loves debate and

controversy, though he keeps his stronger opinions to fairly private gatherings since it falls in his twelfth house. He is a different character to his close friends, to whom he can let out his really unique, highly individualistic inner self.

His real success is yet to come in life. He has tremendous endurance and will keep his career active until well into his seventies.

Severiano Ballesteros
9 April 1957

Sporting the luckiest aspect of all in his chart – a fire grand trine – world-class golfer, Sevvy Ballesteros, was all set for stardom as soon as his feet hit the ground. His mother is the driving force in his career ambitions and he is quite compulsively determined to occupy a public position. However, his father also put more than a little steel in his backbone by instilling a respect for very large quantities of money. He needs to exert total control over his personal finances.

He comes from a rather enclosed family, where his individuality was rather submerged. In later life he may come to realize how much he sacrificed for the family. He has dreams of how an ideal home ought to be, but sadly, he will be disillusioned until he comes to terms with the reality of his emotional life. Somewhere inside he does not feel as strong a sense of identity as he might, so he probably undervalues his success. This has the double-edged effect of making him strive even harder, creating yet more success but with a similarly hollow feel.

With Pluto in Leo strongly aspecting his Sun, he has a powerful side to his personality which likes being influential. He hates being told what to do. That, coupled with Saturn on the other leg of the grand trine, can produce a rather melancholy streak. At times he feels very much the outsider and can be quite obsessive about avoiding crowds. He covers most of these rather less glamorous sides to his nature with a seemingly good-natured bonhomie. Jupiter in Virgo makes him look relaxed with close companions, though it can also produce a side that worries interminably about almost everything. He fears failure to a surprising degree, and tends to veer between supreme optimism and deepest pessimism in estimating his chances of success. Like most successful personalities, he has the ability to push himself fairly ruthlessly when required.

With Venus close to the Sun he oozes charm and could, surprisingly, if given the chance, be extremely lazy. Venus and Jupiter in his chart give him a passive streak which fights bitter battles with his hard-driving need for success and money. But he does enjoy parties, being complimented and flirting.

With Saturn in the fifth house, he is extremely serious about his leisure. Children he will either have late in life or he will regard as a heavy responsibility. He will not find it easy to be relaxed with them.

He is moving steadily on a rising peak in his career which will climax from 1997 onwards.

CHAPTER 4

TAURUS TALENT

IN A NUTSHELL
Dictatorial, musical, animal daft and wonderful lovers.

Film
Shirley MacLaine, Albert Finney, Al Pacino, Sir
Laurence Olivier, Rudolph Valentino, Ryan O'Neal,
Jack Nicholson, Glenda Jackson, Orson Welles, Henry
Fonda, Audrey Hepburn, Candice Bergen, James
Mason, Lee Majors, Shirley Temple Black.

Film Directors
Fred Zinneman, Satyajit Ray, Frank Capra.

Music
Sheena Easton, Burt Bacharach, Cher, Barbra
Streisand, Roy Orbison, Fred Astaire, Stevie Wonder,
Engelbert Humperdinck, Björn Ulvaeus, Tammy
Wynette, Oscar Hammerstein, Irving Berlin, Margot
Fonteyn, Yehudi Menuhin, John Williams (guitarist),
Zubin Mehta, Otto Klemperer, Glen Campbell.

Sport
Henry Cooper, Sugar Ray Robinson, Joe Louis, Chay

Blyth, Steve Cauthen, Sir Gordon Richards, Scobie Breasley, El Cordobes.

Power Figures

Hitler, Marx, Lenin, Eva Perón, Golda Meir, Malcolm X, Lucrezia Borgia, Oliver Cromwell, Catherine the Great, Queen Elizabeth II, Machiavelli, Duke of Wellington, Jim Jones, Maximilien Robespierre, Moshe Dayan, Kenneth Kaunda, Pik Botha, Emperor Hirohito, His Holiness Pope John Paul II.

Writers

William Shakespeare, Richard Adams, Anthony Trollope, Jerome K. Jerome, Charlotte Brontë, Dennis Potter, Joseph Heller, Peter and Anthony Schaffer, John Mortimer, J.P. Donleavy, Morris West.

Art

Brahms, Rossetti, Dali, J.J. Audubon.

Thinkers

Bertrand Russell, Immanuel Kant, Søren Kierkegaard, Pierre Curie.

Medical

Dr Benjamin Spock, Florence Nightingale, Sigmund Freud, Dr Hugh Jolly.

Solid, powerful, rooted, with acres of endurance: there's nothing ephemeral about Taurus top notchers. The Queen is now well into her fifth decade on the throne and shows no sign of flagging. Sir Laurence Olivier, Glenda Jackson, Irving Berlin, Oscar Hammerstein, Burt Bacharach – all entertainers of very long standing. Persistence is what they all share, and the ability to hold their position when all about is changing fast. Taurus hates change!

As an earth sign Taurus loves the earth, nature, animals and the body. The sporting Taurus opts for horses, like Her Majesty, Gordon Richards, and even Albert Finney, who owns a couple, or opts for very physical, tough endurance tests like the heavyweight boxing trio of champions.

Being into the body in a big way sends Taurus either in the direction of the caring medical professions starting with Florence Nightingale, through renowned baby doctors Spock and Jolly, or it produces sensualists. Taurus does like the pleasures of the flesh, eating, drinking, touching and feeling.

Music is another great love. Virtually all great opera singers have at least Mercury in Taurus, and usually Venus as well. Not surprising, since Taurus rules the throat. Musical talent abounds amongst Sun Taurus, all of it standing the test of time.

What most Taureans love best of all, though, is power. Just look at Marx, Lenin, Hitler, Cromwell and Jim Jones of the lunatic suicide cult. What they cannot bear to admit is a power greater than themselves, and it is over-stubborn pride which can be their downfall.

Taurus in Essence

Slow to start, impossible to shift, placid and secure. Think of an enormous bull or an oak tree. That substance is not created overnight. Nor does it blow over in a mild breeze – or a hurricane for that matter. It takes a lot to ruffle Taurus when mature.

As only the second sign of the zodiac, earthy in element, fixed in energy, Taurus shares some of Aries' slightly self-centred infantile approach to life. Me first, or at least my pleasure first. Others' wants and needs come distinctly second, though being around Taurus can be a highly pleasurable experience since gourmet food, hugely comfortable, luxurious furnishing, and good company are usually on the menu.

Sensation is what Taurus love, especially touching. Not necessarily with sexual intent: Taurus just adores that warm, animal feel of being in contact with another human being. But all of the senses are important. Thus Taurus needs music for the ear; nature or art for the eye – colour is paramount; perfume to savour (though Taurus has no objection to the more earthy smells of farmyard and sweaty humanity); the feel of fabric, like velvet, satin, silk; and of course almost anything indulgent to eat or drink. Taurus is the greatest of the gourmet signs.

The practical, material aspects of life are of prime importance. Money and possessions do matter – not because you like filthy lucre for itself, but because security and great comfort are essential. Not normally blessed with a strong imagination, Taurus always likes to take the basic view of life. 'Is it sensible? What is the practical use?' Not very self-analytical, Taurus probably doesn't see much purpose in reading all this. 'I am what I am, I don't want to change, so why stop to question and think?' is a standard attitude.

Possessiveness and even – dare one say it – greed can sometimes be a problem area. Taurus does not like letting go; not, like Cancer, because it fears the pain of separation. It just likes to control, to possess, to accumulate. Constipation, in its physical and psychic form, is a negative Taurus trait. The consequence is that life can turn toxic, blocked, bloated. It is crucial that a flow is maintained; what comes in has to be let out again.

The positive end of that ability to hold on through thick and thin is loyalty. Taureans make the best of friends, often shouldering a ton of griefs and problems. 'Boundlessly wide, sustaining and caring. Calm and still. Reliable and genuine': the I Ching in its second hexagram sums up the second sign's most admirable qualities. Not designed to lead, but to wait for guidance and follow.

Where Aries is all start and no finish, Taurus is all about endurance in the long term, often needing a fairly assertive partner to get the starter motor kicked into gear.

Relationships based on too much give and take are not highly recommended. Not much is allowed to interfere with what they want, or their method of doing it. 'Taurus rules OK' is the motto; even over their partner's affections which they regard pretty much as their personal property. But as the solid foundation for a secure home, there is none better. Warmhearted, affectionate, physically demonstrative, and very down to earth.

Positive Traits

Practical, reliable, patient, adept in business, basic, down to earth, persistent, determined, single-minded, placid, calm, sensual, tactile, affectionate, security-loving, stable, loyal, have good taste, are musical, adore luxury, strong willed, will acquire and accumulate money, have stamina beyond sense.

Negative Traits

Possessive, lazy, self-indulgent, boring, static in their opinions, inflexible, unoriginal, greedy, resentful, obsessed with routines, unanalytical, materialistic, awkward, dull, angry, cruel, none too clean, gross, throw tantrums, have terrible taste, are insensitive.

Taurus' Winning Streak

Horses for courses. Pick the three thousand mile race – it's more your style. If at first you don't succeed, don't change tack, change horses or change race, just keep plugging on. Look at Cher. She wanted to be a movie actress. For years everyone kept refusing her parts, laughed at her ambitions. She was a singer, not an actress, but her persistence paid off. She got the first part and won awards for the talent she always knew she had. Not being over-sensitive is sometimes a huge asset.

The heavyweight boxing ring is more your arena than the china shop. You don't try to duck the punches, because you aren't that flexible, but you do have the courage to stand there and endure through to the fifteenth round.

You have an instinctive feel for reality – so head in directions that allow you to be practical. You are in touch with nature, animals, and the human body. If you feel life is stuck and meaningless, go and look at the trees, talk to the cows, or take up gardening as a hobby. Even pot plants will help. You aren't designed to be a totally concrete urbanite. Your sense of security, stability and strength can be the anchor for more restless, fly-by-night souls.

Taurus as Lovers

On the purely physical level there is none better. Sensuous, sensual, a master of technique and tactic. Interestingly, India, from whence came the Kama Sutra of the one hundred and nineteen different positions, has her Moon in Taurus. You will be wined and dined to excess by a Taurus lover, cosseted in billowing couches, and seduced amongst satin sheets. Or at least that's what they would like to do if they could afford it. Sounds wonderful? It is at the start, but it is very, very physical. After a while it can become a touch gross. The trouble is that Taurus don't think you love them if you aren't making love to them. Your affection has to be tangible. Even Joan Collins is quoted as getting

45

weary of Warren Beatty's continual needs for physical nourishment when they were a twosome years ago. Guess what? Aries he may be, but his love planet Venus is in Taurus. Less evolved Taurus can be a touch animalistic in approach, none too fastidious about hygiene, and downright cruel if their needs aren't met.

Taurus Get On With

Those who don't interfere too much with what Taurus wants! And those who share their practical outlook on life. Virgo, as the adaptable earth sign, is a good companion, and Capricorn's earthy achieving initiative also goes down well, though the latter combination might lack spark and humour.

Aries will provide Taurus with a real sparkle and drive which is needed, Sagittarius can give enthusiasm but is probably too impractical to suit in the long run. The other fixed signs of Leo and Aquarius, and Scorpio share far too much stubbornness to meet with the bull's approval.

Air and earth sometimes have problems finding a point of contact but more sophisticated Taurus share many of Libra's tastes – both being ruled in astrology by Venus, the planet of Aphrodite and beauty. Gemini is too restless, ditto Pisces. At a pinch Cancer could share homes, though the sulks could be years long if fights flare up. Both are quite resentful signs.

Taurus as Children

If as a parent you thrive on excitement, your miniature bull will make your teeth ache with impatience – so slow, so seemingly dull, so placid. You cannot pressure them into moving faster than they want to. All the lovely surprises you spring on them just make them suspicious and sulky. They hate unpredictability!

But think of all the projects you have left unfinished

as too boring. Hand them in junior's direction. Give them a cuddle while you are at it and they will plod on for ever sorting out your unfinished business.

Give them rabbits, hamsters, and pets to look after, a corner of a tub to grow plants in – and, most importantly, a secure environment. Then all will be well.

They may stay young for an inordinate length of time. Boys stay cute well into their middle years. They tend to be late developers, but often what they mature into is well worth the wait.

Taurus as Wives

On the practical level their credentials are immaculate. Sensible, down to earth, like food, like furnishing comfortably, really tuned into baby's physical needs, not at all worried by the messier side of life. So far, so good. They will be the mainstay of the home, providing a secure base – admittedly for themselves, but they don't mind you and the family sharing it.

Problems start cropping up if their jealous side surfaces and you want free space to do your own thing. Even more problems crop up if you have the audacity ever to expect them to do what you want, unless of course it coincides with what they want. Then all is plain sailing.

Taurus as Husbands

Useful round the house, even more useful round the garden, and could even be persuaded into keeping the odd edible livestock if space allows. Will provide a solid base for home and family that will last a lifetime, and a great deal of warmth to fill it.

Younger boyish Taurean husbands are amazingly cute, if a touch irresponsible. They tend to be looking for mothering and fairly voluptuous wives. Taurus does not like wispy women – they need substance in all things, and comfort. Bones sticking out and sparsely-fleshed frames do not turn them on.

Over-obstinate Taurean husbands can be quite cruel. It's no mistake that Hitler was one. There is a nasty side to the sign which comes with that insensitive, unimaginative streak. The less evolved variety often don't know they are hurting people; they just blunder on worrying about their own wants.

Taurus as Bosses

Can be tricky. Look at all those dictators in the list. Absolute submission is the only requirement they have. If you like doubling as a punch bag or a doormat, you might quite enjoy the heavy hand of Taurus wielding the power.

In fact, most of the trouble comes from Taurus interfacing with the boss above more than the minions below. If you know how to keep dictators happy they can be OK. They just don't like rivals or superiors!

Taurus as Slaves

Curiously, can be not bad, domination and submission being two sides of the one coin. Power-hungry maniacs often start life in humiliatingly low positions. Taurus can keep its head down below the parapet for long stretches if necessary, then suddenly one day the coin flips over.

Favourite Saying

'I can't see the point in doing that/thinking about that.'
'I won't move!'

Taurus and Money

Excellent combination. Taurus worries about the long term, only does what has practical value, adores accumulating wealth, and the nicer possessions of life. Only a problem if you are trying to part them from money.

Taurus Towards the Millennium

Forging good close relationships at home and at work was the test of the mid-1980s to mid-1990s, with Pluto in Scorpio. Shaky partnerships did not stand up to the strain and disappeared, but those which weathered the storm emerged strengthened. Enormous changes in your whole philosophy of living were ongoing between the late 1980s and mid 1990s. The 1994/1995 Eclipses pose key questions about your life's direction. This is the great turning point of the decade for you. Thereafter you are sailing through uncharted waters, certainly on the career front. Nothing will be predictable or boring! You are plunged in the last five years of the century into an intense investigation of the paranormal and everything which lies beyond reality.

Queen Elizabeth II
21 April 1926

Born a mere four hours after the Sun changed sign into Taurus, the Queen is truly on the cusp. There is, however, no doubt about her strongly Taurean nature. She adores animals and the countryside, has enormous staying power and courage, and can be very stubborn. But she could never be happy just rearing racehorses, as is sometimes remarked. Her Sun falls in a highly mental area of her chart. Her thinking processes are razor sharp; she can assimilate huge quantities of information. With Mercury in Aries close to explosive Uranus, she isn't slow about fighting back when the situation merits!

Saturn in Scorpio on the Midheaven, which produces her immense devotion to duty, would have fitted her for high executive office anyway, no matter what the family background was. Margaret Thatcher also has Saturn in Scorpio. Both Her Majesty and Mrs T. share that slightly grim, unrelenting attitude to their responsibilities.

With a close Mars Jupiter aspect in tolerant, humanitarian Aquarius in the chart area of personality, the Queen is ideally suited to mix with all races, creeds, colours, and religions. Difference in cultural background increases her interest.

Though her tastes in food and drink appear simple for Taurus, she does have a real love of luxury, of art, of the good things of life. Venus in artistic Pisces gives her an inbuilt appreciation of paintings and music.

Her emotional life is highly sensitive, fairly secretive. With Capricorn on the horizon when she was born, and thus her Ascendant sign, she likes to put up a serious, dignified face to the outside world. Public displays of affection are frowned on.

The Queen's Moon is in regal Leo, giving her an instinctive appreciation of the grandeur and pomp of her life. Mars Jupiter also turns pageantry into a real thrill.

Cher
20 May 1946
Fear and distrust are part of the driving forces of singer/actress Cher's life. With Cancer rising and a first house Saturn, she approaches other people cautiously at first meeting, always doubtful about how far to open up. Her seemingly friendly eleventh house Taurus Sun makes her want to be outgoing, but it is held down and moulded by a powerful Mars Pluto contact so she knows smiles are only skin deep.

Her childhood must have contained a great deal of anxiety, so she brings into her adult life expectations that she will be disliked or humiliated, especially by men. She has resolved that problem by taking the power into her own hands and being top dog herself now, with younger, weaker boyfriends.

Her chart is similar in part to Madonna's, with the same formidable, rather 'unfeminine' determination to be the only one with their hands on the reins of control.

The body, naturally, is Cher's area, being Taurus, and she controls even that, by altering her physical shape according to fashion. She adores the better things in life, and has a truly staggering capacity for earning the kind of money she needs to be indulgent beyond common sense. Mars and Pluto in Leo in the second make her an unashamed materialist. She wants to own, to possess and to have absolute dominion over her personal finances. On top of that, she feels she will never be loved if she does not work to achieve.

On the softer side, she has an idealism about love and romance that leads her into truly lyrical episodes in her life. She needs a close mate for security and will sometimes opt for safety rather than passion. Her dream is of a huge, happy family home full of people, preferably beside running water or a lake.

Her career will go from strength to strength, getting into a phenomenally successful period from the mid 1990s onwards for about ten years.

Jack Nicholson
22 April 1937

Taurus, the sensualist, is more evident in Hollywood actor Jack Nicholson. With Sun, Uranus and Mercury all in the earthy sign at the high point of his chart, he doesn't care who knows it either. Indeed, he goes out of his way to project the playboy image.

A real law unto himself with Jupiter in opposition to Pluto, what he wants he makes pretty sure he gets. No wilting wallflower, he holds strong convictions and much prefers others to bend to his way of thinking.

Venus in Aries makes him upfront in making his fancies known. Any lady who caught his eye would not be left in doubt. With the Sun at the height of the heavens at the moment of his birth, as was the case with many celebrities, he has a strong desire to be a public figure. He was destined for an artistic career and a rise in social status, and was drawn towards a way of life which allowed him to be independent. Life in the civil service would not suit him. Despite that steadfast Taurus Sun, he needs constant excitement and travel.

His long-running on-off relationship with Anjelica Huston was left uncommitted because of his 10th house Sun. It gives him a fear of total intimacy because he senses that deep inside himself, there is not a real person at home. Once Saturn crossed his Descendant in the early 1990s he had to take on more responsibility in close relationships, and that coincided with the birth of his child and marriage. His career is on an upward spiral for a considerable time to come.

CHAPTER 5

GEMINI GIANTS

IN A NUTSHELL
Communicators, comedians, pop singers and split personalities.

Film
Clint Eastwood, Gene Wilder, Michael J. Fox, Brooke Shields, Joan Collins, Marilyn Monroe, Judy Garland, Carrol Baker, Virginia McKenna, Sir Ian McKellen, Tony Curtis, Malcolm McDowell, Rupert Everett, Stan Laurel, Christopher Lee, Peter Cushing, Vincent Price, Errol Flynn.

Film Directors
James Ivory, Sam Wanamaker, Tony Richardson, Ken Loach.

Music
Paul McCartney, Barry Manilow, Tom Jones, Kylie Minogue, Jason Donovan, Prince, Marvin Hamlisch, Lynsey De Paul, Dean Martin, Nancy Sinatra, Julie Felix, Bob Dylan, Curtis Mayfield, Gladys Knight, Pat Boone, Anita Harris, Al Jolson, Cole Porter, Benny Goodman, Nick Rhodes, Noddy Holder.

Sport
Jackie Stewart, Bob Champion, Robert Sangster, Andrea Jaeger, Alwin Schockemohle, John Newcombe, Jacques Cousteau, Jesse Owens, Zola Budd, Steffi Graf, Pat Cash, Björn Borg, Joe Montana.

Politics
George Bush, John F. Kennedy, Henry Kissinger, Lord Carrington, Che Guevara, Mario Cuomo.

Royals
Duke of Edinburgh, Prince Rainier, Ex-King Constantine of Greece, Duchess of Windsor (Wallis Simpson), Queen Victoria.

Writers
Margaret Drabble, Salman Rushdie, Jean-Paul Sartre, Thomas Hardy, Thomas Mann, Françoise Sagan, Brigid Brophy, Arthur Conan Doyle, Saul Bellow, Arnold Wesker, Athol Fugard, David Hare, Ben Johnson, W.B. Yeats, Walt Whitman.

Art
Richard Wagner, Igor Stravinsky, Dürer, Pietro Annigoni, Gauguin.

With Mercury, the winged messenger of the gods as ruler, Gemini could be expected to produce wordsmiths, communicators and more than its fair share of the highly voluble. Newspaper offices in particular, and indeed any of the communication businesses, attract Geminis by the horde, with Virgo as the next favourite sign – also ruled by Mercury. With Sagittarius, it is the favourite sign also amongst lawyers who, like journalists, are never lost for a word!

Eternally curious, Gemini has a reputation for

superficiality. Most Geminis know a mite about a million things. Even in music the Gemini taste tends to run to light, mass appeal rather than anything too deep and intricate, though there are a couple of notable exceptions to that. So it's not surprising to find amongst their midst the pop singers, especially those with a message to communicate like Bob Dylan. Their work tends to be popular rather than purist, creating intense interest for a short period of time. This is a reflection of that tendency to stay on the surface and look on the bright side of things. But don't be misled – there is a strong awareness of the dark side of life. Most Geminis have a bleak, black side. Poor Marilyn Monroe is an extreme example of that contradictory split – half blonde pretty butterfly, the other half deeply despairing. Most Geminis, however, attempt to stay on the bright side and reject the darkness.

A few Geminis fall totally over into their black side, which is why there is an unholy collection of murderous villains. Neville Heath, for example, sadist and murderer noted for crimes too horrible to describe. He was hanged.

Gemini in Essence

In a word – split. The myth for Gemini is the Twins, the glyph is the Roman numeral II. And never the twain shall meet. In the myth the divine twin is never present when the human twin is about, and vice versa. It is the central fear for those who bear the sign that they can never quite connect with the other in a relationship. Always there is a sense of a desert, a wasteland in partnerships.

Part of it is because Gemini is an Air sign, a mental, rational, thinking animal – not emotional at all, in essence. It is Gemini's strength to be detached, to be able to stand back and observe, to gain perspective, not to be committed and tied, but to be constantly on the move looking for new angles, new possibilities. When it comes to relationships, those most positive Gemini assets can prove a drawback. Geminis need to be free, at least in spirit, to fulfil their needs for variety.

Gemini's favourite occupations are reading to pick up information, thinking, and most importantly of all, talking. Nothing is more attractive than a stimulating chat where knowledge is paraded, and titbits collected for future use. Don't think of it as a desperately intellectual sign – it isn't. Gemini is too restless to stay put long enough to become a specialist in anything, but for breadth of knowledge you can't beat them.

Unless sunk in the depths of their dark side, they make great party and dinner guests – witty, bright, full of jokes, highly adaptable. By the end of the evening they will have chatted to almost the entire guest list. They love variety in other people but curiously they can be quite intolerant, often racist. The part of themselves which they are split off from within, they will hate outside as if it didn't belong to them.

Discipline and endurance are obviously going to be a problem with such a grasshopper sign. So career choice is crucial. Don't head for routine, never-changing, long-running projects. It's why communications suits the sign: no two days are ever the same in journalism, television or indeed law. New faces, new cases, new stories; never a chance to get bored. Often Gemini's work has an air of mystery surrounding it: an air of the intangible, sometimes an air of dishonesty! But there is always something you can't quite pin down.

That wonderfully detached sense of perspective does create in relationships a chilly, or at least remote, insensitivity to other people's feelings. Not being well into their own emotions, Geminis often can't empathize with anyone else's feelings. Often too much emotion makes Geminis jumpy. They like a dry, spacy atmosphere, not too much dripping water about the place.

Friends they like to be assertive, go-get-em types, lovers are expected to be socially presentable, and spouses to be ever-cheerful. Other people need to be stable round them, as their sense of values changes daily.

Brothers and sisters are always a significant issue in Gemini's lives. They are not always hugely close, indeed often quite difficult inter-family relationships are around, but they can't be ignored, usually. Frequently the sibling carries energies which the Gemini won't recognize in themselves and hence dislikes in those closest during childhood. So have a good look!

Constant travel, complex family relationships, communication – those are the three life areas ruled astrologically by the third sign. Investigation of the rational mind often helps to ground over-airy Geminis, curb the restlessness, and improve family relationships immeasurably.

Positive Traits

They are communicative, have a flair for writing and language, are adaptable, versatile, witty, busy, spontaneous, amusing, creative, original, great flirts, have perspective, are detached, diplomatic, tactful, curious, smart, clever, funny, curious, not too clinging.

Negative Traits

They are restless, changeable, cunning, inconsistent, two-faced, nervy, highly strung, unable to relax, superficial, gossipy, rebellious, childish, verbose, dishonest, cold, unemotional, insensitive, unable to relate, fickle, idiotic, unfaithful.

Gemini's Winning Streak

You have a head like Encyclopaedia Britannica, the curiosity of ten thousand cats, and enough nervous energy to run the country's power stations. Others may accuse you of lacking integrity because you change so radically and quickly, and you can compromise. Most situations in life demand some compromise; many demand real chameleon qualities, which you have in abundance.

You are the adaptable sign *par excellence*, so you need a niche where constant excitement, variety and change are the order of the day. Taurus, Leo and Scorpio, never mind Aquarius – all the fixed signs – create trouble because they can't bend. You can flip around like a jack-in-the-box.

Others don't like your rebellious streak. That's their problem – old stick-in-the-muds. Your nonconformist nature allows you to be inventive, original, creative with ideas, and if one idea doesn't work out, there are several hundred more where it came from.

You have the ability to meet and chat brightly for a brief time to a wide variety of contacts. Relationships are not your strongest point, but work and socializing don't require deep passions.

Gemini as Lovers

Assuming the bright side is uppermost, that sparkling, stimulating bubbly Gemini makes for a wonderful social companion. Even in private, the conversation never gets stuck. But after a while you might be forgiven for wondering if there is anything substantial behind all those babbling words.

Geminis don't like coming down out of their heads and their vocal cords – the emotions and the body are not two of their favourite areas. It's a hoary old cliché in astrological circles about the Air signs, but contains a grain of truth none the less – they'd rather be thinking about it or talking about it, than actually doing it. So if you like your love deeply emotional, heavy with passion, and always physical – Gemini is not your sign. Nor are you theirs.

What Gemini really adores is a relationship with lots of space, an attentive ear at its disposal, and a bright mind who can feed back titbits of entertaining information. And most certainly not too much emotional anguish. Gemini just doesn't like feeling too much. If you get emotional, it pulls them into their emotions – and they run. So hopefully they pick partners who are equally laid back and restless, then everyone stays happy.

Fidelity, it has to be said, is not Gemini's most outstanding virtue – some, obviously, do settle, but really it isn't in the nature of the beast. They like to roam at parties and flirt outrageously. Often it means little: just a new audience for the old patter.

They aren't always hugely sensitive to your feelings either – they can be quite cruelly detached at times, but usually it isn't malicious. It's just that they don't want to be pulled into empathizing with your grief or anguish. Their own dark side is so painful that they need to stay out of it.

Gemini Get On With

Being highly adaptable, they get on with almost everyone, over short periods. Their first preference is probably for other Geminis, or Libra, another Air sign. Next comes Sagittarius, their opposite sign but full of fiery enthusiasm, equally restless and always cheerful, and even more importantly interested in ideas. Aquarius is accepted for its mind, but on sufferance: its obstinacy is a drawback.

Geminis like Virgos because of their bright, analytical

minds and ability to compromise when necessary. They quite like Aries and Leo for their bouncy confidence.

Taurus and Capricorn are too earthy, materialistic. They feel stodgy, almost coarse to Gemini. But the Water signs give most problems, Scorpio especially – all that deep, dark, intense passion is much too emotional. Cancers cling like limpets and are so supersensitive that they complicate life with emotional tangles Gemini can't understand.

Gemini as Children

Keep their boundless curiosity well fed. Never keep them short of books – get them to join several libraries. Send them off to the local museums and Natural History exhibitions. They may have to be pressured into learning more concentration than comes naturally, but don't expect miracles. They need variety.

Try to teach them a little about honesty – they can be a touch vague on that score. Try to sort out their more antisocial traits when young. Gemini's problems worsen through life if not resolved early. Teach them techniques to relax – all that constant movement revs them up like a car with the automatic choke stuck. They end up with ulcers if they can't unwind.

Don't expect your little butterfly grasshopper to conform – they like to maintain their sense of themselves as separate beings. Drown them in emotion and too much physical contact, and they'll flee back to their books.

Gemini as Wives

Loves entertaining, loves socializing, but would much prefer to read a book than clean the house. She's fine if working and the domestic chores can be shared out – then she doesn't feel too tied.

Don't expect endless emotional and physical support through illnesses, ailments and the less romantic patches. She will cheer you up enormously with chirpy patter, but poulticing boils and holding sick basins hold few attractions.

You need to take her away on constant trips, not just once a year, but several times a month, here there and everywhere. And she will be enchanted when you go away on your own for brief spells: too much togetherness weighs her down.

Gemini as Husbands

If you are of a jealous, insecure temperament, Geminis are not recommended as mates. The male of the species is especially fickle; some quite faithless. The infidelities won't usually matter much to him – just extended flirtations. Anything that gets too heavy he'll ditch.

Career and money are often areas of unreliability. Some are hugely successful, but nothing in Gemini's life stays the same for too long. So you need to prepare for all contingencies. Don't expect a steady, ever-responsible, ever-reliable breadwinner – he ain't.

Many male grasshoppers never grow up – if the idea of a cute little boy appeals to you, then Gemini is your sign. But be warned, the appeal can grow thin in middle years when your needs for excitement have calmed down.

On the plus side, you'll be the envy of wives who are wilting with boredom in the midst of utter security, total fidelity. As Felicity Kendal remarked 'Do you really want a man you are completely sure of?' You won't ever be bored with a Gemini spouse and the risk factor will keep you on your toes!

Gemini as Bosses

If you can ever find them, really quite fun. But they are

never where they are supposed to be. Geminis don't fit happily behind desks: they wander. They will always be interested in your point of view, and just adore having you in for a chin-wag.

Don't always expect them to play fair – there is a highly devious side to Gemini at work. Expect to drown in memos: they spin them out like confetti.

Gemini as Slaves

On the surface, not bad at all. All that adaptability, lack of integrity and thus lack of their own sense of values, lets them fit into what you want at the drop of a hat. Will run errands happily, because it keeps them on the move. But underneath it all – beware. They will dump you in the ditch if the opportunity arises, and skip merrily away.

Favourite Saying

'Did you know that the natives of the Limpopo River were really descendants of Siberian fur trappers?' 'Why are you crying? It's silly, and quite unnecessary.'

Gemini and Money

Disorganized and never quite clear what the rules and regulations are about. Will cut corners. They understand the theory of money; it's the practice they find boring and distasteful.

Gemini Towards the Millennium

The chaos in your emotional life which the triple conjunction of Saturn, Uranus and Neptune in Capricorn wreaked through the late 1980s fades into memory, happily, by the mid 1990s. Now you have shaken the patterns of the past off your back the future looks brighter, more expansive. Joint finances also settle by 1995. A career high which starts in 1994 stretches to 1996. Close partnerships become more intense and quite transforming after Pluto's entry into Sagittarius in 1995. The future is quite uncharted, but you intend to ride the waves to find your fortune. Moments of glory are on offer in 1998, as your talents are given full recognition.

Barry Manilow
17 June 1946

With his Gemini Sun close to highly individualistic Uranus, Barry Manilow was guaranteed to put his own unique stamp on whatever he did. He is happy to be himself, even if that appears eccentric, and even happier if he can pioneer his own style of music.

His is an Air, Water, Cardinal chart so he thrives on ideas, on chat, on giving out emotion. He is achievement-oriented and is extremely restless. With a shortage of Earth signs in his chart, he is likely to ignore practical things like eating sensibly, resting and exercising. He'll function best if there's always someone beside him to take care of the basic essentials.

An emphasized Jupiter in close aspect to romantic Neptune and the Moon, which rules emotional needs, gives him a rather sugary, sentimental public image, and he attracts an almost religious adoration. Underneath it all there is a great need for love, affection and acceptance. He likes to do things in the grand style with Mars in Leo, and to be feted by his adoring fans.

With Mercury in Cancer he is very sensitive to criticism, although he hides his deeper vulnerabilities away from the public gaze, thanks to Venus in Cancer. Much of his creative talent stems from Venus close to Pluto, allowing him to combine drama with music. It can also give great depth to the passions, but in such an airy chart these are likely to be handled with care and channelled into his singing.

Joan Collins
23 May 1933

Hollywood's greatest soap star has, appropriately enough, the chart of a social butterfly. Venus, planet of love affairs, frivolity and self-indulgence, falls in fickle Gemini beside her Sun. So she likes variety in her romantic and social life, has a keen wit and sparkling conversation, and relates exceptionally well at a surface level.

With both Sun and Venus emphasized in her chart, she has a strong, powerful personality, and likes to be centre stage with the spotlight on her. To lesser mortals she may be overpowering. Bette Davis and Marlon Brando share that heavy Sun emphasis and it creates larger-than-life personalities that command attention, though not always respect and love. Ultimately, it brings a high potential for leadership, fame, acclaim and honours. Popularity at a personal level does not always arrive early on.

Her Moon is in earthy, acquisitive Taurus, which helps to stabilize her emotions and means that she values money in the bank. She has a great deal of persistence in domestic matters, which was very obvious when her daughter was hurt in an accident. She didn't leave her bedside till Katy recovered. That's Taurean stubbornness in her mothering lunar side.

Although the Gemini in her nature keeps her moving constantly, she is not by nature impulsive. Her chart is almost all Air and Earth, and lacking in spontaneous fire and nurturing water. At times she can appear detached and quite cool.

The life she leads now was part of her childhood dreams, born as she was in the midst of the Depression years when the warmth and comfort she craved was in short supply. With an amazing group of planets – Mars, Neptune and Jupiter – in Virgo, the sign of hard work, it was clear that one day she would turn her dreams into reality through her own efforts. Neptune is romantic and rules the movies; Mars adds a dash of glamour and attraction to the high life; and Jupiter tops up the energy and enthusiasm. She has never taken 'no' for an answer. What she wants, she has had the confidence to head straight for.

Ultimately she may move behind the cameras to an executive position.

George Bush
12 June 1924

George Bush's rather grey image comes in part from his Virgo ascendant which makes him look prudish, modest and rather pinched. Also a chilly Moon Saturn conjunction, and a childhood in which duty came before pleasure, undoubtedly stopped the free flow of his spontaneity. He desperately wants to be noticed and admired. He feeds off publicity, but finds close intimate contact with people difficult. His ambitions always came before romance.

His saving grace in what must have been a very unpredictable marriage, where he demanded total freedom to work as it suited him, comes from a highly amiable Jupiter in his fourth house. He really does warm to a huge family gathering, adores having his grandchildren around him and loves nothing more than an open door policy where friendly neighbours may pop in for supper.

His Gemini Sun gives him the capacity to cope with a million different details at once, and he thrives on a full schedule since his boredom threshold is low. He keeps his vague, impractical streak well hidden. Neptune in Leo tucked out of sight could have given him addictive problems earlier in life, but he probably kept his head down and became addicted to success instead.

He is not good at holding a steady course over a long period because of a highly restless Sun Uranus Jupiter T square. He constantly wants to be on the move, after new and different adventures. Long-distance running was never his style.

A Venus Pluto contact in Cancer has always given him the charm to connect with exceptionally influential people. But he has a secretive, less sunny side that he keeps well out of sight. High level conspiracies would keep him very happy in his days at the CIA, since he thrives on deep strategy and sleights of hand. He is not all he seems.

CHAPTER 6

CANCER CLAN CHIEFS

IN A NUTSHELL
Matriarchs, mother complexes, prophets and pioneers.

Film
Meryl Streep, Harrison Ford, Gina Lollobrigida, Ingmar Bergman, Sylvester Stallone, Donald Sutherland, Kris Kristofferson, Mel Brooks, Tom Cruise, Ken Russell.

Music
Ringo Starr, Carly Simon, George Michael, Cat Stevens, Buddy Rich, Debbie Harry, George Hamilton IV.

Sport
Gary Sobers, Mike Tyson, Pam Shriver, Tony Jacklin, Nick Faldo, Ilie Nastase, Arthur Ashe.

Royals
Princess of Wales, Duke of Windsor, Prince Michael of Kent, Prince William, Dalai Lama, Sultan of Brunei.

Writers
Ernest Hemingway, George Orwell, Herman Hesse, Tom Stoppard, Iris Murdoch, Elizabeth Kubler Ross.

Art
Degas, David Hockney, Gustav Mahler.

Business
Stavros Niarchos, Peter de Savary, Richard Branson, H.J. Heinz II, Joseph Wedgewood, John Jacob Astor, John D. Rockefeller, Pierre Cardin, Teddy Tinling, Hardy Amies, Elizabeth Emanuel.

Pioneers
Sir Edmund Hillary, Roald Amundsen, Emmeline Pankhurst, Alfred Kinsey, John Glenn.

Matriarchs
Rose Kennedy, Nancy Reagan, Barbara Cartland.

Matriarchs and founders of world-famous family dynasties are the hallmark of Cancer, sign of the crab, the Moon, the home, and Mother. Not that Cancer mothers are necessarily warm and cuddly: Rose Kennedy may have produced the most politically potent family of twentieth-century America, but she is tough rather than tender. The Cancer femme is formidable. Look at Nancy Reagan and Barbara Cartland – hardly shy stay-at-home types. Even the Princess of Wales has a reputation for putting her foot down hard in domestic situations. That said, for all their forthright qualities, the family is crucial. They need that sense of continuity.

Amongst male Cancerians, founding a family dynasty is often an ambition. Look at the household names – Wedgewood, Heinz, Rockefeller, and Astor. The family business is the thing.

Cancer is ruled by the Moon, a very feminine energy, but one which sensitizes Cancer people to public taste, so they quite intuitively know what will be successful.

That very feminine intuition makes for good prophets. Cancer's feel for the unknown takes them to outer space like John Glenn, up Everest like Hillary, to the pole like Amundsen. Or it makes them pioneers. They want to explore unknown territory, break new ground . . . especially in new ideas which concern society and humanity. Pankhurst pushed for a new view of women, Kinsey explored current sexual practice. All of them had a profound influence on the public at large.

The Duke of Windsor typified one kind of Cancerian male – the little boy lost still looking for a mother substitute. Cancer men often marry exceedingly strong women – or stay unmarried. The United States, not surprisingly, is Cancer – a very matriarchal society, oversensitive about its macho image, because deep down there is a feeling of inadequacy in American males. America's vast overweight problem comes from the Cancerian fetish about eating and nourishment, often as a compensation for feeling unloved. Italy, country of the Mother Church and ruled by the always-at-home but ever powerful Mommas, is also Cancer. Italian males have much the same problems as American ones. Mother never let them grow up.

Cancer in Essence
Cancer's prime motive in life is self-protection, staying hidden. So they can be the most irritatingly mysterious of people, never revealing what you really want to know.

The glyph for Cancer is the crab – hard-shelled but extremely soft and vulnerable underneath. Although it is the first of the watery emotional signs, Cancerians can often seem remote and chilly. That's just the defence system in action. Like crabs they always move sideways; they sidle in when least expected and nip opponents round the ankle.

Ruled by the Moon, which also rules the tides, Cancer's emotional moods follow the same ebb and flow. One day outgoing and charming, the next withdrawn and distant. High tide, low tide. Full moon, no moon. The lunar realm is the feminine realm – both are fickle, at times beyond rational sense. Cancer is all of that.

Cancer needs to share, to relate, to be close, to cling, to empathize. To do all of that, they need very thin psychic skins: then they can really merge with others. But the problem with thin skins is it makes you hypersensitive, and really not well prepared for the hustle and bustle of the nasty, rough world out there. So they need an almost impenetrable outer defensive shell to scurry behind when life looks like hurting them.

Above all else, Cancer is the sign which feels pain – emotional pain – most exquisitely. Especially the pain of separation, which is why they let go with such reluctance. Cancer is not possessive like Scorpio, because they want to hold power over the other. Cancer is jealous and possessive because they can't stand the thought of not being attached to the other – like a limpet, or a baby at a mother's breast.

Mothers or mothering is a major issue with Cancers. Many Cancerian men have real mother complexes and stay attached to their childhood homes for long after it is healthy. Often they leave their natural mother merely to marry an equally stalwart substitute.

Home is important partly because it is a place of security to retire to in moments of stress, and partly because family and roots give Cancer a feeling that they are attached to life, and to the past, which they value highly.

A very creative sign, because it has such close contact with the emotions and thus the whole unconscious realm of the imagination, it produces artists really in touch with the needs of their time. Not only can Cancer empathize with their closest family: they also have a sympathy for the needs of society as a whole.

Often it is called a midwife sign rather than a mother sign. It helps in birth, rather than creates of itself. Creative art is often about preparing the arena, and then just letting the unconscious flow out of its own accord. Letting the muse take over was the old poets' way of writing; Cancers often do that with life. They know that we are basically out of control, small ships tossed about on the sea of life. So they just let go and drift with the currents.

Their creativity is often reflected in their acute dress sense. Dress designers appear in the list of the famous Crabs as well as those who entertain the public with their outfits. Cancer has good taste in spotting anything to do with the feminine realm, whether it be clothes, home decor or food presentation.

They tend to have opulent tastes, be critical of siblings, want to be somebody quite grand, attract a hardworking spouse, be ambitious careerwise and attract artistic, wealthy friends.

Positive Traits
Kind, sensitive, sympathetic, have a powerful imagination, strong parental instincts, are protective, shrewd, thrifty, emotionally resourceful, pay off debts, cautious, subtle, compassionate, give comfort and nourishment, tune into others' feelings, are secure, sensitive to atmosphere.

Negative Traits
Are touchy, snappy tempered, moody, changeable, untidy, unforgiving, too easily flattered, self pitying, overdependent, clinging, defensive, too sentimental,

passive, jealous and possessive, stuck in the past, hoard old belongings, old-fashioned, not physical or passionate, want to be wanted too much, sulk, have no sense of humour, especially about themselves.

Cancer's Winning Streak

That wonderful ability to get inside other people's skins, and find out what they want, allows you to give them what they want. On a career level, it means you can work in a variety of public jobs; anything that brings you near people or allows you to put forward ideas about current trends and tastes is good news.

Your colourful imagination and good taste can be put to good use at home around the family or anywhere around the dress industry, fashion, interior decor, and food. You hate letting go – so go where people need someone to lean on, and cling to, such as the caring professions. Or go where tradition is valued and respected, and the continuity has to go on. Elizabeth Kubler Ross pioneered work with the dying which was of enormous benefit both to the patients and to those left behind. Cancerians should stop worrying about not having enough distance or perspective on life. Your strength is not that you think; it is that you feel, you connect, you relate.

Cancer as Lovers

Wonderfully attentive to your needs, they will create delicately romantic settings at home for your intimate candlelit dinners. Both sexes cook well, will tell you how tenderly they feel for you. They just adore being close to you, and cuddling you.

Passion they understand as being with you. They will leave you to make all the running. Cancer tends to sit passively and wait – except if you threaten their security. Then they act with lightning ferocity.

Physical sex on the whole they can take or leave. If you offer comfort, closeness, tell them they are wanted and you won't ever leave, they will smile with sweet charm and be satisfied.

The trouble comes when you have had enough and want to leave – tenacious is an understatement. They cling, they manipulate, they make you feel guilty, and they cry – oceans of tears. And don't try to two-time them either – laid back and tolerant they are not. All that sweet charm turns to vindictive jealousy. Green eyes glare at you.

As with all things Cancerian, there is the up side and the down side. The up side can be very attractive – but it comes at a price!

Cancer Get On With

People who feel and people who are nice, gentle and genteel. Start with Pisces: emotional, kind and often need nurturing. Libra they incline towards because Libra always think of other people's needs, though Cancer has a sneaking feeling they are a bit chilly behind the caring. Both signs are quite snobbish. Scorpio, though emotional, is far too manipulative to suit the Crabs. Cancer women are often attracted to the 'little boy looking for a mother' signs of Gemini, Sagittarius, and to a lesser extent, Aries, which tends to be too brash and insensitive.

The Earth signs go down well. Virgo they like because of their helpfulness and tact; Taurus attracts because it provides security and protection. Capricorn is acceptable because it provides money and social status.

Sometimes they yearn for Leo, but the king of beasts tends to be terrified of all that emotion and escapes posthaste. Aquarius they understand least of all.

Cancer as Children

Never laugh at them. Their fear of ridicule verges on the paranoiac. When it happens they snap their little shells shut and retire into a massive sulk. They are masters of the art of passive resistance: if they don't want to do something, no amount of wheedling, cajoling and bullying will shift them. Just wait for the tide to come back in!

They cling like limpets to home, and invite all their little friends round to play rather then venturing out. You despair of ever cutting the apron strings. You must! They have to learn to leave the past behind at some point.

Let them learn all the domestic skills – cooking, sewing, interior design. Let them develop their creative side. When they eventually leave they will entertain you royally in their magnificently decorated, supremely comfortable adult home. And you won't be short of grandchildren!

Cancer as Wives

Custom built, though you may have trouble preventing them turning you into one of the children to be mothered along with the rest of the brood. As far as home comforts are concerned you'll be in seventh heaven – food prepared with skill and love, presented with flair; the interior decor tasteful, creative and all with an eye to comfort.

If you equate wives with families, then Cancer is top of the list. But you have to like strong women and be prepared to sacrifice your independence. Families are all about togetherness!

Cancer as Husbands

If they marry, and not all do, they make excellent fathers. Sometimes if they marry, they also make wonderful sons for their wives. The Duke of Windsor did. But you have to be very clear at the outset how detached he is from mother's clutches, otherwise what you get may not be a husband at all.

The mature Cancerian male, who has successfully negotiated his rite of passage away from childhood, is very good news indeed. Thoughtful, kind, caring, responsible, interested in providing a beautiful home and happy to be in it. Probably also highly successful.

Cancer as Bosses

Good as far as providing all the in-house benefits of sick pay, free coffee in the canteen, and extended maternity leave are concerned. They have a tendency, however, to throw tantrums. Doesn't always have a sense of humour if you make mistakes that reflect on him/her. Needs to feel you appreciate their role as super broody hen. Will soak up flattery quite naively. Will never ever forgive you if you leave and will never ever forget you did – so don't go back ten years later expecting to be welcomed.

Cancer as Slaves

Sulky, in a word. Whining, self-pitying. If you take away Cancer's mothering role, really a form of power, then they revert to clinging children and need looking after. They will look after your every comfort at one level, but the amount of looking after they will require in return may make the exercise counterproductive.

Favourite Saying

'How could you hurt me like that?' 'I won't do it!'

Cancer and Money

Resourceful, acquisitive, needs it to provide beautiful home filled with objets d'art so will work hard for it;

pays off debts. A touch erratic when it comes to handling other people's money.

Cancer Towards the Millennium

Close relationships have been in turmoil since the late eighties with Neptune creating misunderstandings, Saturn chilling the romantic atmosphere and Uranus making for explosive tensions. All in all it was a miracle that some relationships stood the strain. Inevitably, some did not. Until 1995 a lack of intimacy is almost inevitable. Feelings of loneliness and isolation are not pleasant, but they are teaching lessons about self-sufficiency which will be extremely valuable. Love will be less intense after 1995, though moments of high excitement will occur until the turn of the decade. Joint finances are hardly straightforward through this decade either, with shortages until 1995 then a roller coaster period of feast and famine. However, the real crisis/turning years were 1991/1992. Then you made the decisions which will stay with you for at least twenty years. Heavier career responsibilities are in evidence from 1996 for four years.

Princess Diana
1 July 1961

With her Cancer Sun shining brightly above the horizon when she was born on a summer evening, Princess Diana was guaranteed to be a public hit. The sense of fun, of intuitive understanding of current trends, and of her role as an entertainer all shine out of her birth chart. She could have been an actress.

Her ascendant sign is Sagittarius, ever cheerful, ever colourful, ever on the move. Or at least, that is the face she puts up for the outside world. Inside, Mercury in Cancer will produce someone who is supersensitive.

Most birth charts and personalities show

contradictory traits. Princess Diana's major conflict is between that home-loving, traditional Cancerian side and a super-independent Aquarian streak. This can prove a tricky combination, especially for someone in the constant glare of the limelight who will find it difficult to enjoy the freedom she needs. The split in the family in her mid-teens would not have helped in learning how to make the best of those two traits. She veers between the highly solicitous Cancerian mother and the independent public figure who has to travel away from home frequently and continuously. Some of these contradictions she acts out on her body, feeling the need to get back to almost girlish slimness after her pregnancies – right to the opposite extreme, away from the maternal.

She can push herself too hard, which contributes to her weight loss. Her chart has an extraordinary cluster of the heaviest planets together, necessary for someone who constantly has to face dangerous situations: Uranus, which is explosive, Mars quite violent and Pluto connected to ultimate force and power. This combination does make people slightly accident-prone.

Harrison Ford
13 July 1942

Born at the time of the Cancer New Moon, Harrison Ford is highly emotional and enormously self-protective. He has a nose for what the public wants, chooses his movies with real intuition, but is determined to maintain his privacy behind solidly-maintained defences. He is like that other sea creature – an oyster – who only ever feels safe if its shell is firmly shut!

With Jupiter, Mercury, the Sun and the Moon all at the midheaven of his chart, there was never any doubting that he would head straight for a career with a high public profile which would bring him honour, high regard and success. He will become a pillar of the community in later years.

He has one of the indications of genius in a highly bunched chart and is certainly good at focusing in on whatever interests him with tenacity and even fanaticism. But with only one Earth sign in his chart, he is not remotely practical or grounded. He tends to be swung around by his moods more than is obvious from the outside. He has great compassion and kindness. In other circumstances he could have been a healer.

Being a New Moon person, he has less need of close relationships than most so can shut himself away when working to the exclusion of all else though, of course, being Cancer he will need to have a family around for comfort some of the time. He gives the impression of being cold, but is in fact shy with rather low emotional self-esteem. He is uncomfortable around too much feeling since it pulls him around.

He can be extremely tough in group situations, exerting quite a powerful influence on friends and colleagues. His leaning towards a view of life that sees beyond reality will bring him into contact with mystical and paranormal interests. His career is good for another twenty years at least, with plenty more successes to add to his collection.

Meryl Streep
22 June 1949

The most public face with the most private personality, Meryl Streep typifies Cancer's great paradox: how to stay private while in the full glare of public attention and adoration. With Venus in Cancer, she is deeply sensitive about her home and emotional life. It also confers on her that delicate femininity she uses to such stunning effect in her acting.

Her Moon falls in materialistic, security-minded Taurus. She needs financial stability to be happy and adores all the home comforts. She also typifies the Cancer 'femme formidable'. She is no shrinking violet when it comes to getting her own way. She knows what she wants and does her best to get it.

Her meticulous attention to detail and to learning the authentic accent for her different film roles comes, curiously, from close contact between Saturn and Mercury. She uses this feeling to its best effect, learning more than she might otherwise have done. With aggressive Mars close to Mercury in Gemini she loves debate, argument and controversy. She is intensely curious and could, later in life, take up writing.

Her intense and individualistic personality makes it difficult for her to relax with workmates and the general public. Her desire for perfection, to achieve greater things, means she is her own hardest taskmaster.

Dominating her chart is a rare configuration known as a 'yod' or finger of destiny. Those who bear it often have a fated change of direction in life. The Duchess of Windsor had one, so has Mrs Thatcher. The twist of providence this indicates will allow her to broadcast her own social message to the masses. She will have as strong an impact on society at large through her ideas as she has at present through her acting.

CHAPTER 7

LEOS IN THE LIMELIGHT

IN A NUTSHELL
Lionhearted leaders, limelight lovers and quick-witted communicators.

Film
Peter O'Toole, Martin Sheen, Dustin Hoffman, Sean Penn, Robert de Niro, Shelley Winters, Robert Redford, Roman Polanski, Jill St John, Robert Mitchum, Susan George, John Huston, Cecil B. De Mille, Ilya Salkind, Stanley Kubrick, Peter Bogdanovich, Arnold Schwarzenegger.

Music
Mick Jagger, Sarah Brightman, Madonna, Whitney Houston, Oscar Peterson, Buddy Greco, Count Basie, Debussy.

Sport
Vitas Gerulaitis, Willie Shoemaker, Robin Cousins, Chris Dean, Ben Hogan.

Royals
Queen Mother, Princess Anne, Princess Margaret, Marina Ogilvy.

Writers

Bernice Rubens, Jacqueline Susann, George Bernard Shaw, Beatrix Potter, Lord Tennyson, Shelley, Emily Brontë, Robert Bolt, V.S. Naipaul, Alexandre Dumas, Aldous Huxley, Carl Jung, Sir Walter Scott.

Trendsetters

Coco Chanel, Yves St Laurent.

Centre stage is where Leos feel in their element. Above all else it is the sign of the actor, the entertainer, the showman. People with this sign have a larger than life personality. Napoleon may have been mite-sized, but there was nothing small about his ambition. Mick Jagger strutted arrogantly to a success unheard of before or since in the pop business. Cecil B. De Mille's best known movies were *The Greatest Show on Earth* and *The Ten Commandments*. Modesty, moderation, and caution don't feature noticeably in Leo's life plans.

Pride of place is important to Leos, which is why Princess Margaret, and in her younger days, Princess Anne, found being a minor royal difficult. They need to be centre of attention, not the fourth most important person there. Princess Anne has flourished since she found a niche which is totally hers.

The grand lifestyle attracts Leos. Jackie Onassis, who sacrificed respectable widow's weeds for a marriage dripping with wealth, was exhibiting Leo's need for colour, importance, and richness. Not for nothing is Leo's colour bright gold. Yves St Laurent and Coco Chanel are names that call to mind the elite. It's brass and celebrity status that count with Leos, not necessarily the breeding.

The Queen Mother, another Leo, always appears in eye-catching, humming bird-shaded outfits, that most people would find difficulty in wearing. She carries it off to perfection.

Leo in Essence

Warm hearts and generous natures. Leo at its best stands for everything that makes life worth living: joy, love, children, creativity, and growth. Look at the positive benefits of the sun – it brings heat, light, and colour, causes the earth to flower, and puts humanity in a better mood, unlike its opposite the Moon which is dark, hidden, grey, and depressed.

Leo is the Sun. Leo personalities shine forth, usually with brilliance, entertaining, uplifting, leading, putting everyone else in better humour. Leos feel passionately and openly, and convey all that warmth to everyone in the vicinity. They are enthusiastic, creative, dramatic, expansive.

Self-confidence seems to ooze from every pore and it can be very contagious. They love children, both their own and other people's, but not in a sentimental, emotional way. They are just for life – and children convey that spontaneity, bounce and fun of existence, that Leos find so attractive.

Leos come from the heart. Often referred to as the sign of burning passion, deep down Leo always thinks every problem would disappear if the love of their life turned up. 'One day my prince/princess will come!' And thereafter, it's happy ever after, up the golden staircase into the heavenly clouds. They aren't, as you might gather, one of the more realistic signs.

They are attached to home and family, but not domestic. They just like the sense of having a den of their own, full of mini cubs, looking up to them with respect, admiration and love. And they will defend home and family against outsiders with a ferocity that is unrivalled amongst the signs. They are truthful and straightforward, sometimes too much so for their own good. Often they are too trusting: they expect others to be equally honest.

That's the good news. If it sounds too good to be true – listen to the debits. Leos may give light but they do rather see themselves as the centre of the animal kingdom, with everyone else as satellites, revolving round them. They don't regard themselves as being like other people. They are bigger and better than everyone else. As long as you remember that, give them due admiration and more importantly praise, then the sunnier side of their nature will shine for ever all over you.

They do tend to be a touch egocentric. The negative side can produce people who are pompous and overbearing, and give you the feeling there's a hollow centre in that over-blown ego. There is. Reject a Leo, humiliate them, cut them down to size and you'll hear the sad hiss of a hot air balloon deflating. And a sorry, crumpled sight the end result is. Inside they are quite insecure.

Leos need their pride and an arena in which they can show off. Though they are very heart-centred, in their younger days they tend to be insensitive to the needs of others. So relationships don't always work well. They also have a very nasty habit of expecting others to do as they want, while insisting on having total freedom themselves. 'You do what I want and I do what I want.'

They have double standards, in fact, though they are disarmingly open about it, unlike some of the other signs, most notably Scorpio. Leos have a barefaced, brass-necked cheek about their double standards that quite takes your breath away, makes you giggle and prevents you being as murderously angry as you intended to be. They can be blissfully generous and always give impressive presents, which helps to balance some of their less attractive traits. Leos are meticulous with money, possessive at home, outgoing at parties, serious at work, like freedom in close relationships, like to travel abroad and up the social ladder.

Positive Traits
Are generous, creative, enthusiastic, good organizers, broad-minded, expansive, have a sense of showmanship and drama, are earnest, sincere, fashionable, romantic, self-confident, have a sense of humour, are outgoing, demonstrative, loyal, very sexy, proud, warm, passionate, adore children.

Negative Traits
Are dogmatic, bullying, pompous, snobbish, intolerant, patronizing, conceited, vain, ostentatious, insatiable, childish, indolent, tense, angry, judgemental, insensitive, naive, showoffs, inconsistent, hot-tempered and noisy with it, can't stand humiliation, overbearing, very sulky.

Leo's Winning Streak
Your overwhelming need for acclaim and admiration suits you to be precisely that – someone who holds others' attention. Either you entertain them, or you rule as king/queen over them. That way, you get what you wanted, and they can enjoy your talents in return.

Forget all about the meek inheriting the earth. That was probably written about a Virgo. You need position, power, authority and enough brass to look flashy. Flaunt your wares, your talents, your personality. The King of the Beasts doesn't stand in queues looking subservient.

Love, luxury and life itself are what give you incentive, spark, buzz. You may be insecure at times, but you don't usually lack confidence. So start expanding. Your creativity starts with you.

Instead of a novel, a painting or a sculpture, start on

yourself. Your love of children nourishes you and helps them. If you start by acting out what you want, however self-consciously, one day it will all fall into place naturally.

Leo as Lovers

Leos have the steadiest sex drive of all the signs, the warmest heart and the most generous nature. That's if you get a good 'un, or are a good 'un. So there's much to recommend the species as a love companion.

Being a fire sign, the wooing, winning and seduction are carried out with style, romance and all the trappings. But at least Leos linger on thereafter, which is more than can be said for Aries. They are very loyal and have a strong sense of honour and chivalry about their responsibilities, even in a passing affair.

All that imagination needs fantasy to stoke the fires of passion, so the love can't be too earthy, mundane and realistic, or Leo feels it all a bit beneath their dignity. They love to have partners on their arm who impress the world at large. The King must have his Queen, and vice versa. So although Leo will demand a pride of place, you need to come up to scratch or Leo's reputation will suffer.

They cannot stand rejection in any form, so require fairly delicate handling at all times. Don't expect equal tact about your sensitivities, or you may not be disappointed.

Leo Get On With

Courtiers, audiences, respectful admirers, slaves, and children. Sagittarius is possibly their favourite – enthusiastic, but bendable to Leo's will. Virgo lacks the sparkle but gives such excellent service, they match well. Libra is liked for their thoughtfulness, superior social sense, and excellent taste. Capricorn also brings social advantage and money though is really too serious for Leo. Aquarius, curiously, gets on well with Leo. I say curiously, because both are fixed, stubborn signs and Aquarius is highly detached. Two Leos together is extremely noisy; the tussle for pride of place quite awesome.

Gemini is too restless and not straightforward enough for Leo, and the water signs are all a bit of a mystery. Cancer is as night to day to Leo, Scorpio devious, and, worse, power-hungry. At a pinch a vague Pisces will do – as a slave or a stray waif.

Leo as Children

If you happen to be a self-effacing parent, you may squirm with embarrassment at their unashamed demands for applause and attention. Let them show off. They instinctively know that life's a stage – and they are rehearsing for the lead role. And prima donnas are usually very well paid!

Their tantrums will undoubtedly be noisier and more theatrical than anyone else's. Just put in ear plugs and rest assured that life will knock some sense into them when they leave home. Be prepared, though, to be abandoned fairly callously when they go. They will only learn the finer feelings of care for their elders later on in life.

Let them entertain the neighbourhood kids. For one thing, it keeps them out from under your feet; for another, an audience is vital to their sense of identity. They need to see a mirror reflection of themselves in the response of others. Otherwise, they don't know who they are.

Leo as Wives

Not wonderfully domestic as far as mundane chores go, but excellent organizers. Doubly excellent with children, whom they will raise with vigour and enthusiasm. Their warmth and personality mean home will never be dull or chilly, though it may be a touch volcanic at times. For Leo ladies are passionate about most things. When their foot goes down, the floorboards shake. They love throwing lavish parties, will decorate the pad in an extravagant, eye-catching manner. They are a real asset on social occasions, and will make you the envy of the other husbands.

Minor drawbacks include expense. They like a lavish lifestyle and if they don't work, you will have to provide the wherewithal. They are also quite demanding – so if all you want is a quiet life with a meek wife, forget Leo.

Leo as Husbands
Can be a pillar of strength, sexiness and sustenance or alternatively, thoroughly overbearing. Generally, a bit of both. Older Leo men are infinitely preferable to the younger variety, who tend to blunder about tramping all over your more delicate spots. Once life has taught them about compassion for others, they can be a real treat.

They do require their place at home. They need a den of their own, and at times an undue amount of admiration, respect etc. from the rest of the household. They also tend to tell jokes very loudly at parties. If you get embarrassed easily, keep him supplied with good joke books. He is honest and will stick to his duty through thick and thin because his honour demands it.

Leo as Bosses
It suits them down to the ground! They ooze pleasure at having a throne to sit on. They are lovely to work for and generally give generously of money, time and attention to underlings. They can be stubborn. You

won't change their views easily. On the other hand, they won't go behind your back if they disagree with you.

Leo as Slaves

Could not be worse. Without doubt the least-fitted sign to be tramped under heel. They sit sad and dejected, with no incentive for life at all. They sulk in a leaden fashion and grow lazy, usually fat. They are not a pretty sight.

Favourite Saying

'But I am better than everyone else.'

Leo and Money

Leos don't want money for its own sake. They leave that to the trading classes. They want it for what it buys in luxury, position, and admiration. You can't furnish a place on 25p. So they are generally resourceful at earning, and hugely indulgent in spending. They want the biggest, the best, the flashiest, the most showy. They often talk well for money. Though can be vague about spending other people's . . . but since they are basically an honest sign, they come to no harm.

Leo Towards the Millennium

Work and love were the great bugbears of the first half of the 1990s. The end of the Capricorn triple conjunction which first threw chaos into your career plan in the late 1980s continues to create mayhem until 1995, but by that time you have got used to taking life on the run. Enormous changes at home in your emotional life stretch right through this decade. Saturn in Aquarius until 1995 brings chilliness and separation to relationships. Thereafter, Uranus and Neptune bring independence and more than a touch of confusion into your love life.

Pluto in Sagittarius from 1995 to well into the next century will force you to face in depth how much of a power struggle has been ongoing in your intimate relationships. You could develop real skills in handling large quantities of money at this point. 1999 is a major turning point in your life.

Princess Anne
15 August 1950

Princess Anne is eminently suited for a public life of influence and power. When she was born mid-morning, the Sun was approaching the height of the heavens and appears in her birth chart in her area of career. To live out her personality she needs high public office, unlike, for example, Prince Charles who is more of a home-lover.

She exhibits all of Leo's pride and sense of high-born nobility. In her younger adult days her brash, slightly overbearing temperament caused trouble. Like most Leos she ages well, and as she learns to tap her compassion in helping others she will mellow further. With Pluto beside the Sun at the peak of her chart she is probably destined to become something of a legend in her lifetime.

She carries a strong sense of duty towards her mother. Her own emotional nature was affected by the inevitable partings in early childhood. She worries a great deal about the Queen. Much of her own personal role she sees as being for the Queen's benefit rather than her own.

Marriage cannot have been easy for her, at the age she was. Those who carry similar chart placings to hers tend to marry later in life or have multiple marriages. With Libra on the ascendant, the face she shows the world is light, bright, colourful. The older she becomes, the more tact and diplomacy she will show.

Although her Sun is in sunny, open-hearted Leo, that strong Pluto contact gives her a secretive Scorpio streak in her nature. This often comes to the fore because an extremely determined Mars in Scorpio was almost exactly on the horizon when she was born. Mars is a great fighter, usually a sportsman; her prowess on horseback and persistence as a jockey are evidence of this. But in Scorpio it can also brood over slights and hurts. She enjoys children though is not a soft, emotional mother. Her own offspring will bring her distinction. Her travels around the world for Save the Children Fund draw on both her caring instincts and need to see for herself what's going on.

Since 1982 she has been forging a lifestyle which better suits her individuality.

Like the rest of the younger Royals she comes to greater prominence in the early 1990s, suggesting a major change in position then. She is at her most successful and productive between the ages of forty-five and sixty.

Madonna
16 August 1958

Madonna does not have the overwhelmingly ambitious, determinedly materialistic sort of chart that megastars frequently have, where success and money are the only goals. On the contrary, she acts out of a very private space as if she was compelled to display her psychological complexes to the world at large. Her flamboyant Leo Sun close to eccentric, highly individualistic Uranus is hidden away in a dark but creative place in her chart. The real Madonna always stays protectively hidden. Her inner world is a place full of great riches, arcane monsters and a considerable quantity of chaos. She needs to steer clear of people at times, to calm her volcanic emotions down.

With aggressive Mars in square to her Sun, she has strongly masculine traits, likes to be in charge and is quite frightened of powerful men. Success may be her weapon as a defence against the men whom she fears might push her around. Her temper is awesome, especially when she feels her wishes are being ignored. She cannot stand interference in any form.

Her childhood was obviously a struggle with not much emotional support and little chance for her to develop more feminine traits. She lacks water in her chart, suggesting she distances herself from her emotions which at times threaten to overwhelm her. She also lacks air so she finds it difficult to be detached and in particular to see herself clearly. Curiously, she also lacks cardinal signs so she is not great as a self starter, though marvellous as a stayer. She has the stamina of an ox.

Settling down to a happy, comfortable home life will never be easy for her, since she has no experience inside herself for it. But her career looks set for a good long run, albeit with some mighty upheavals along the way.

Arnold Schwarzenegger
30 July 1947

A curiously unearthy and unphysical personality comes across in the chart of the world's most famous male body. Terminator and Conan the Barbarian he may be on screen, but in reality he has trouble staying connected to his flesh and blood. A sixth house Moon also indicates that his emotions often affect his body fairly dramatically, weakening him more than one might imagine.

He has no problems at all staying in touch with money. His chart shows similarities with Steven Spielberg's. Both obviously had it in mind early in life that they were going to be very rich, and they carried this vision with them into their career. Both are slightly mean and quite compulsively determined to maintain control over their personal wealth.

Schwarzenegger has an amiably bland image, stemming from a Cancer ascendant with Mercury and Venus perched on it. He is talkative to a nervy degree but oozes charm, sympathy and sugary sentiments. He hides away a highly intolerant, rather explosively irritable streak, which he fears might mark him out as someone rather unstable, though it is this simmering volcano within him which he obviously uses to such good effect in creating his screen roles.

He had to sacrifice a fair amount for his childhood family. Staying with them meant losing his identity. He dreams now of a beautiful, always harmonious home life and is likely to have attractive children who will bring him good fortune. He adores children and will always be easy company for them.

CHAPTER 8

VIRGO VERBALISTS

IN A NUTSHELL
Workaholics, communicators, critics and surprisingly sensual.

Film
Sean Connery, Jeremy Irons, Richard Gere, Lauren Bacall, Sophia Loren, Ingrid Bergman, Raquel Welch, Greta Garbo, Jacqueline Bisset, James Coburn, Ben Gazzara, David Soul, Peter Falk, Linda Gray, Anne Bancroft, Larry Hagman, Pauline Collins, David McCallum, Elliott Gould, Herbert Lom, Nicol Williamson, Peter Sellers, Oliver Stone.

Music
Michael Jackson, Chaim Topol, Jessye Norman, Jose Feliciano, Brook Benton, Barry Gibb, Itzhak Perlman, Van Morrison, Kenny Jones, Elvis Costello, Loudon Wainright III, Freddie Mercury, Alan Jay Lerner, Buddy Holly, Sir Peter Maxwell Davies, Sir Frederick Ashton, Leonard Bernstein.

Sport
James Hunt, Jimmy Connors, Captain Mark Phillips, Arnold Palmer, John Lloyd, Clive Lloyd, Stirling Moss,

Tom Watson, Yves St Martin, Barry Sheene, John Curry, Malcolm Pyrah, Bernhard Langer.

Royals
Prince Harry, Duke of Gloucester, Hon. Angus Ogilvy.

Writers
Shirley Conran, Frederick Forsyth, Martin Amis, A.S. Byatt, Michael Holroyd, Fay Weldon, D.H. Lawrence, Roald Dahl, Mary Stewart, Agatha Christie, H.G. Wells, William Golding, Edgar Rice Burroughs, Christopher Isherwood, Lady Antonia Fraser, Malcolm Bradbury, Dr Samuel Johnson, Jorge Luis Borges, Jessica Mitford. Goethe, Tolstoy, O. Henry, J.B. Priestley, Siegfried Sassoon, Dante, Stephen King.

Achievers
Mother Teresa, Sir Isaac Wolfson, Sir Bernard Lovell, Aristotle Onassis, John Paul Getty II, Zandra Rhodes.

With Mercury, the winged messenger of the gods, as ruler of Virgo, you would expect communicators to loom large in the ranks. And the media is fairly infested with Virgos in newspaper offices, the film business, television and publishing. They are the go-betweens, who carry the message to the masses. The task is the priority, not their egos. Most Virgos, if anything, could do with a touch more flamboyance and chutzpah.

Words especially are their forte. The great and weighty writer like Tolstoy, Dr Samuel Johnson, and the lighter, brighter variety like Frederick Forsyth, all exhibit Virgo's meticulous eye for detail, and rare ability to observe the minutiae of human behaviour.

Sex symbols are there in surprising abundance. Sean Connery, Sophia Loren, Raquel Welch. There are also gossip column headliners like the eight-times-married Alan Jay Lerner, and in their day Ingrid Bergman, and

Peter Sellers. These are all a testament to Virgo's earthy side. The surface appearance of controlled respectability hides very passionate depths, though not all Virgos make the descent to find them.

The depths of sensuality plumbed by D. H. Lawrence and, in the popular genre, *Lace* by Shirley Conran is, I suspect, more a head exercise than anything plucked from the roots of their living experience. In the case of the latter, one might hope so! Virgo stands back, observes and communicates.

Virgos love to serve their fellow humans, not because they are desperately humanitarian. They just like being useful to other people. Thus Mother Teresa, who works tirelessly and selflessly for others, is Virgo. The great philanthropist Sir Isaac Wolfson, and actor Sean Connery, have both in different ways, given back some of their wealth to help others, by setting up charitable trusts.

Virgo in Essence

Forget everything you have read about Virgos being just what the office manager needed to keep the accounts and filing system in order. Many journalists are Virgos and a more untidy, rabble rousing, Rabelaisian lot you never met, so chaotic with money they are the despair of their bank managers, expense-signing bosses, and spouses. Forget also the tired clichés about Virgo virgins. The original models for the sign were the goddess of fertility and the temple harlot, who was both holy and a whore.

First and foremost Virgos are about work and service to others. Hence Mother Teresa. What is important is the task in hand, not the fame, success or glory that goes with it. Watch them at parties. They never feel entirely at ease just enjoying life. The nagging suspicion is always there that they should be doing something –

handing round the crisps, chatting up the wallflowers, even washing the dishes. Or standing on the periphery of things, eying the proceedings, and giving a running commentary. Wonderful as observers, analysts, critics, that sense of detachment and fine judgement is also their tragic flaw. Hint to Virgos – life is not a spectator sport or material for a good novel! Emotions do not need, and certainly don't like, minute dissection and analysis. Other people do not always need, and more often do not like, your criticism and advice!

Virgos should stop moaning and get into life. Unwrinkle their fastidious noses, pull on their wellington boots and splosh happily through the mud with everyone else. Experience it, feel it, then they blossom. But they do have to descend to the depths, and get into the murkier side of life to do it.

Domestos may kill all known germs but that negative Virgo over-sanitized approach, if allowed to run unchecked, destroys the taste and fun and flavour of life as well. That's where you get the old-maidish spinster Virgo in both sexes – their guts have shrivelled and their blood dried up through underuse. Men if anything are worse than women in this respect. They can be unattractively fussy.

The more full-bodied approach has much to offer Virgos. They are an earth sign and although their sensuality is buried fairly deep, once contacted it offers rare pleasures. Dionysus, the god of ecstasy and orgies, is connected to this sign. Many prostitutes, curiously, are born under Virgo. Maybe not so curious when you think of it as a sign of service – they offer their bodies to satisfy the needs of others. Sadly, it is at the expense of detaching their own emotions and enjoyment.

Where all Virgos are very attached to their bodies is through their interest in health. Never call them hypochondriacs! It's just common sense to have the bathroom cabinet stuffed full of potions, lotions and remedies, the kitchen groaning with vitamin pills and sensible food. Mention a health worry to a Virgo and you'll drown under the weight of good advice.

Sexy they may be if you dig deep, but self-contained they almost always stay. They don't absolutely need to relate from the depths of their soul, the way some signs like Scorpio and Libra do, being such a fussy, perfectionist sign, as far as others are concerned. Virgos won't drop their standards and settle for whatever is around as a partner, which is why they often stay unmarried till later in life. It's not that the perfect mate turns up then: just that life has usually managed to get the message across that perfection doesn't come in human form!

Positive Traits
Sensible thinkers, practical, down to earth, hard working, honest, efficient, sexy, warm hearted, good with small animals, clean, healthy, meticulous, dependable, adaptable, discriminating, helpful, independent, understanding, happy to work out of the limelight, intelligent, keen on quality.

Negative Traits
Moan endlessly, nag, nitpick, dole out unwanted advice, act as doormats, are shrewish, talk about nothing other than work, are obsessed with detail, worry about everything under the sun, are over-fastidious, lack personality, lack humour, are nervy hypochondriacs, are frigid if not asexual, chaotic, self-pitying.

Virgo's Winning Streak
Virgos enjoy hard work, are keen to see the job properly done and have no false pride. Look at the Virgo stars.

Virtually all of them have built their careers on hard, conscientious slog. Pride never got in the way of practicality. If you feel your Virgo timidity and doormat qualities are holding you back, then look at the positive strengths of humility. You can get down there and get on with the task in hand. Leo couldn't do that; their need to be grand can be a terrible burden, and a drawback. You don't need top billing; you can fit into most situations and adapt to most personalities. You'll be there long after the prima donnas.

Virgo as Lovers
Depends completely on whether they have ventured out into life yet. If they are still on the sidelines, forget it. They will criticize your performance, your clothes, your grammar and the colour of the wallpaper; give you very unromantic advice about the workings of your intestinal system at quite the wrong moment, and analyse the emotional content of your relationship to the point where it freezes.

But if they are living, laughing Virgos with blood coursing through their veins you won't do much better. In public they are well behaved and slightly demure, with an appearance of breeding and quality. In private, they are warm, earthy, sensual, highly adaptable to your likes and dislikes, thoughtful, amazingly supportive through illnesses and below-par patches, kind to your dog/cat/budgie, and usually good cooks.

Virgo Get On With
Most people. As a mutable earth sign, they are adaptable and practical, so will put up with virtually all the signs if necessary. For preference they like the other Earth signs – Taurus and Capricorn, also hard workers. They like Gemini for its mental qualities, Libra for its niceness, Sagittarius because it is cheerful. They

feel sorry for the confusion of Pisces and treat them like a pet. Scorpio is a touch too heavy and intense for most Virgos, and the highly egocentric signs like Aries and Leo grate slightly. Perhaps there is some envy there: meek Virgo can't understand the cult of personality for its own sake. They'd never dare!

Virgos work exceptionally well with other Virgos. They each respect the other's conscientious streak. However, double Virgo marriages are in danger of becoming too dry and in serious danger of analysing themselves to divorce. Virgos need someone to make them laugh at themselves once in a while, someone less ordered, a little wild.

Virgo as Children
Can be the meekest, tidiest, most irritatingly goody two-shoes you ever met, so obedient you long for their wicked, rebellious side to appear. Or they can be wildly chaotic and impractical: it just depends which end of the spectrum is showing. The opposites are closer than you think! Virgo's obsessive tidiness often springs from a fear of the total chaos which is running under the surface. They tend to be restless, to like doing things constantly, talking, tidying, fussing, fidgeting. Relaxation won't come easily.

Give them tasks to keep idle hands busy. Set them projects awash with detail. Try to get order into the chaos if it exists, but also teach them life is there to be enjoyed. Don't worry if their friends seem to use and abuse them. They will learn sooner or later that being trampled all over isn't the same thing as service.

Redirect their critical faculties away from yourself. Teach them that perfection is an ideal, not a possibility.

Virgo as Wives
On a practical level, excellent. Good cooks, nurses,

small animal minders, clean, tidy, hard working, efficient, practical. They will make endless lists, keep the house in shipshape order, and the family's health will be watched with an eagle eye. Will prop up everyone else's ego, especially yours. Won't worry too much about being ignored. Greatest problem – nagging!

Virgo as Husbands
Impossible to generalize, but needs to be constantly stimulated if not to become boring ultimately. Can exhibit fairly unmasculine traits of fussiness. Needs to be able to laugh, but a good provider.

Virgo as Bosses
Slave drivers! They think everyone is as obsessed by work as they are. Finicky about detail, never really satisfied, not good at delegating, so constantly checking to see if you are doing it right. If you can live with that, they are generally fair-minded, honest and won't dump blame sideways on to you.

Virgo as Slaves
Custom built! But underneath, they will resent it furiously. Will moan behind your back to anyone who will listen. Will be tediously self-righteous when you get it wrong and never let you forget it. Will be subtly disloyal.

Favourite Saying
'I wouldn't do it that way.' 'I told you so.'

Virgos and Money
They aren't materialistic but they love quality, which never comes cheap. So they are much more extravagant than their reputation suggests. They alternate between expensive purchases and periods of frugality. Can be

chaotic when younger. Generally, by their middle years, order has descended on the tax returns, bills are neatly filed and promptly paid.

Virgo Towards the Millennium
The early 1990s were marked by the same emotional upheavals which ended the 1980s. Only by 1995 will peace have reasserted itself. Then certain close relationships will separate or have separated to allow for a new phase of life to begin. Strong relationships will have weathered the storms to come through in fighting fettle. A career surge comes after 1994 but along with it a sense of uprooting. A major home change or even country change could take place within the last half of the decade. 1997 is your year for grasping your life in both hands and making radical decisions. This is your moment in destiny for choosing to live in a different way.

Sean Connery
25 August 1930
The movie star fans lust after, and journalists tread warily around, has little to do with the essential man. With four planets out of the ten in Virgo, including both Sun and Moon, he is in his element at work behind the scenes on the film set. A workaholic, a perfectionist, he pulls his weight as a team member, not standing on his dignity or his ego, though woe betide any slipshod workmates. He isn't short on Virgo's more critical faculties, with Mercury in its own sign.

With the bulk of the planets in the eighth and ninth houses of his chart he is a deep thinker, interested in ideas, serious literature, philosophy: a much more mental man than his macho image suggests.

His very formidable physical presence comes from a Cardinal Grand Cross on the chart. A rare configuration, it denotes a life of struggle on which the individual builds his success. It certainly straightens the spine and strengthens the character from an early age, but easy it ain't. At times he feels as if he is carrying the burden of the world on his shoulders. Life is a bit of a battlefield.

As with Mrs Thatcher, Saturn was on the horizon when he was born – in his case in Capricorn. So he puts up a defensive exterior to the outside world. He feels the need to build an emotional wall around himself, so he seems a touch austere. Behind his protective front he is shy, very loyal, and happily mellowing with the years.

Jupiter and Pluto side by side indicate he would overcome the poverty of his childhood to gain great wealth, though he retains his frugal streak. One danger for him is Neptune in the eighth suggesting confusion in business finances, and untrustworthy advisors. He needs to be very realistic in this area.

His extraordinarily seductive film image, stemming from that Pluto and a strongly Scorpio feel to his chart, is probably more of a projection than a lived reality. Although he has attracted himself to very intense ladies in life, his own relationship planets Mars and Venus are in the air signs Libra and Gemini. They suggest a man not interested in gaining a reputation as a stud.

Mother Teresa
27 August 1910

Service, sacrifice, humility and hard work – all Virgoan traits which Mother Teresa lives out to the fullest extent. Not only her Sun but also Mars was in Virgo when she was born. Mars is a fairly masculine energy which pushes forward assertively to get things done. She must have struggled long and hard in her early religious training to control her temper.

Most of her energies are in earth – over half the planets were in the Earth signs of Capricorn, Taurus or Virgo at her birth so she is immensely practical, organized, grounded in the body and not repelled by the grosser physical aspects of life. This helps her to nurse those living in the most squalid conditions.

Strangely enough, her chart lacks both fire and water, so she has little native trust in life itself. The only Water sign is Neptune in Cancer. Neptune is incredibly spiritual and Cancer the mothering, nurturing planet, so she lives her emotions out through her religious faith, with not too much imagination to distract her.

What makes her chart outstanding is a rare configuration of planets called a mystic kite, tying together an incredible talent for making things happen in a practical way with a deep sense of sacrifice. That comes from Uranus sitting in Capricorn across from spiritual Neptune.

Her faith drives her on, so does her temper and so does her inner emotional tension. She has an enthusiastic way with words, making her points very forcibly and getting her message across as much by personality as anything else.

With Jupiter at ninety degrees to Uranus, she thrives on adventure and sudden travel. Jupiter in contact with Neptune means she attracts devotion and adoration. Like all visionaries, she tends to build castles in the air and live in the expectation of her dreams coming true. The luck in her chart guarantees she isn't often disappointed.

Her Moon, with all its nourishing, nurturing qualities, carries a significant message for our time since it is tied into the Moon's Node. Her task was not only to be helpful in a practical way, but to inspire those mothering qualities in many others. She was destined to be a woman of our time. Happily, she didn't duck the challenge.

Michael Jackson
29 August 1958

Founding a secure home life in which he holds total control is the main aim of Michael Jackson's life. Certainly he wants to feed the public with the latest fashion in music. His Piscean Moon, right at the midheaven of his charts, marks out his musical talents clearly enough, and his nose for what is in the public taste at any moment. But really his drive is much more inward than outward. He fears being overwhelmed by dark emotional fears stemming from childhood, so he exerts total domination over his feelings and intimate relationships.

With Jupiter in the fifth he has a sunny creative side which adores children, but sadly his Saturnine seventh house causes him to hold back from commitments for fear of the responsibilities involved. He could settle down, though, in later life.

A boisterous, rather eccentric group of Leo planets make him a wacky, creative entertainer, always determined to be seen as the one who is marching to a different drummer. He loathes anyone interfering with his plans and, despite his rather demure Virgo character, he can be explosively irritable if provoked.

He has an active mind, a wonderful way with words and could write if he so chose. With Neptune also in the fifth with Jupiter, he obviously has a magically creative career marked out in the entertainment business. Neptune especially favours music, but it also makes him a romantic dreamer. He wants a lover who is perfect, whom he can idealize. Sadly, in reality he is likely to feel let down by his love life.

His career spans ahead until well into the 2000s.

CHAPTER 9

LIBRA IN THE SPOTLIGHT

IN A NUTSHELL
TV types, public people, sleek women and soft men.

TV
Barbara Walters, Johnny Carson, Clive James, Angela Rippon, Anna Ford, Melvyn Bragg, Andrew Gardner, Magnus Magnusson, Robert Kee, Gordon Honeycombe, Sandy Gall, Mavis Nicholson, Anneka Rice, Judith Chalmers.

Film
Roger Moore, Chevy Chase, Sigourney Weaver, Charles Dance, Walter Matthau, Richard Harris, George Peppard, Donald Pleasence, Yves Montand, Montgomery Clift, Julie Andrews, Diane Cilento, Dame Anna Neagle, Brigitte Bardot, Christopher Reeve, Charlton Heston, Susan Sarandon.

Music
Julio Iglesias, Bryan Ferry, John Lennon, Johnny Mathis, Linda McCartney, Olivia Newton John, Cliff Richard, Max Bygraves, Barbara Dickson, Matt & Luke Goss, Bob Geldof, Luciano Pavarotti, Marie Osmond.

Sport
Martina Navratilova, Jayne Torvill, Ted Edgar, Evel Knievel, Basil D'Oliveira, Eddie Macken, Sebastian Coe.

Politics
Margaret Thatcher, Lech Walesa, Desmond Tutu, Melina Mercouri, Dwight D. Eisenhower, Pierre Trudeau, Mahatma Gandhi, Ramsay Macdonald, Eamon de Valera, Juan Peron, Jimmy Carter, Oliver North.

Royals
Duchess of York, Duke of Kent.

Writers
Jackie Collins, Oscar Wilde, Truman Capote, Gore Vidal, Jan Morris, Lord Alfred Douglas, Harold Pinter, F. Scott Fitzgerald, Arthur Miller, T.S. Eliot, Damon Runyon, James Clavell, Mario Puzo, Günter Grass, John Le Carré, Samuel Taylor Coleridge.

More public personalities are born under Libra than any other sign. TV attracts Libras like a honey pot. At least ten top British TV interviewers, America's two highest paid TV stars, and the last two Director Generals of the BBC, all are Libras.

The world of television provides the atmosphere of brittle sophistication, of detached chitchat, that suits Libra. They like communication, an active social life, status and not too much emotion.

Libra ladies are usually sleek, can be remote, a touch like the Ice Queen. They almost always have quite masculine minds – clear-thinking, incisive, well organized. Margaret Thatcher is an excellent example. She dresses in a fairly feminine, though unfrilly way, but there is absolutely nothing frivolous about how she thinks. Like many Libra women she is her father's daughter, one reason she can more than hold her own in a highly masculine world. Politics and TV suit that slightly hard-edged temperament.

Libra, being the sign of the scales, often crosses over to the opposite to provide the balance. Libras in women's bodies have 'male' minds; with male Libras the reverse happens and typically you find a softer, more sugary temperament: a tribute to Libra's contrariness.

Pop singers, popular light music specialists, and pleasantly familiar household names from acting and variety exhibit the advantage of Libra's emotional detachment – keep it light, keep it colourful and on the surface. Think about other people's likes, because that way comes social acceptance. So it is the sign of the salesman, of diplomats and lawyers.

Libra in Essence

You can forget the myth about Libra being balanced and moderate for a start. Certainly, the scales are Libra's motif. But have you ever tried to balance scales? They're all lopsided at the beginning and just as you begin to even them up, to achieve that precarious state of absolute equilibrium, you overdo it and they unbalance to the other side. That's Libras' lives: aiming for the centre but mainly wobbling between the extremes.

Reputed to be highly diplomatic, they can also be awful troublemakers because they always take the opposite point of view to balance the scales. You say black, they say white. Give them time, and they will also argue for every grey point of view in between. They do like to see all round a subject – endlessly.

Often they are accused of lacking integrity. Partly, they so want to be liked that they will tell you what they think you want to hear. Partly, they tend to shift position depending who is arguing with them. Faced with Labour, they think Tory, and vice versa.

If none of this sounds like Margaret Thatcher – she is more than her public image suggests. But also she has strongly Aries/Scorpio traits in her personality which tend to drown Libra's more placating tendencies.

As an air sign, Libra tends to be fairly detached and unemotional. The standard variety runs the gamut from light and playful to chilly formality. Social convention is more important to Libra than any sign other than Capricorn. Looking 'nice' is where it's at. Unwashed, foul-mouthed hippies make Libras' flesh crawl, or at least their fastidious fingers curl.

Ruled by Venus, planet of Aphrodite, goddess of beauty, Libra is heavily into the aesthetic. Taurus, also ruled by Venus, likes beautiful things to touch, to feel and to possess. Libra, being airy, stands further back. It likes beauty, likes to think about it, likes harmony in the air. Most Libras are elegant and refined in their tastes, except where food is concerned. Then their extravagantly sweet (or creamy) tooth emerges.

Libra can be most delightful company, and can be superb hosts and hostesses. Expect a colourful, tasteful home decorated expensively, if conventionally. Expect your likes and dislikes to be remembered from your last visit. Expect pleasant music in the background.

Curiously for a detached mental sign, Libra is always spoken of as the sign of relationship. This is because it thinks always of the other. Librans need to feel accepted and approved of – so will go to great lengths to ensure their actions fit in with the whims and needs of those around. Sometimes that gives rise to accusations that Librans have no taste of their own, or no integrity: all their actions are merely reactions. There's a touch of truth there, but it isn't a malicious shifting of ground.

The motive is always to please or to balance.

The benefit of all this is a mind capable of seeing a problem from any number of viewpoints, so it gives real breadth. Librans' perspective can be truly panoramic – they see all round the issue. And when they finally make up their minds, often a really fair, just opinion emerges. Time lag can be a problem, though; they do dither! Tiresias, one of the mythic characters associated with Libra, was the only mortal ever allowed to pass judgement on the gods – he took fourteen years to deliver his verdict! But he did gain hugely in insight from the experience. Wisdom is never instant.

Positive Traits

Are charming, harmonious, easy-going, romantic, diplomatic, tactful, idealistic, refined, peaceful, clean, sweet, affectionate, communicative, light, playful, pleasant and relaxing, sentimental, sophisticated, sleek, polite, thoughtful, colourful, musical, sensible, balanced, moderate, *nice*.

Negative Traits

Are indecisive, resentful, snobbish, frivolous, changeable, flirtatious, overinfluenced by others, gullible, lose identity in their partner, seesaw between extremes, cold, insipid, overdependent, not passionate, detached and chilly, unemotional, greasily insincere, too formal, overeat, are too extravagant, and too conventional, argumentative, contrary.

Libra's Winning Streak

That wonderful, all-encompassing charm and ability to see everyone's point of view make you a superb 'people' person. Librans can bring calm to troubled waters, pour flattery out in every direction, and bring even the most vicious enemies to an inkling of insight into the alternative viewpoint. So capitalize on your abilities as a mediator, and a harmonizer. Don't volunteer for an instant-decision situation – you need time to reflect, to walk gently round in circles. Your judgements need time to mature but, like good whisky, the quality improves with age.

Ignore jibes that Libra ladies are unfeminine and Libra men a little too much so. You understand the opposite sex better than any other sign; you can genuinely see things from their point of view. Libra men can make marvellous companions. You revel in convention, in what is popular, elegant, refined, tasteful. So you aren't radical, revolutionary? So what. Society would be in chaos if everyone chose to walk new paths. You help to keep the structure of society together.

Libra as Lovers

If you want wildly uninhibited, very physical passion – don't aim for Librans. But if you want an elegant, sweet natured, agreeable personality at ease in upwardly mobile society who can probably entertain you in their own beautiful home, you may find it here.

Emotion is likely to stay at the light, playful level but the conversation will be sophisticated, intelligent, full of charm and wit. Librans will be ever-thoughtful about your needs – almost too much so – but if you are fiendishly self-centred and not too crass they will give you attention way beyond the call of duty or sense.

If you have any odd preferences in your love life, Libra is definitely not your choice. They are very conventional, won't try different positions in anything, and really like their sex awfully nice and frightfully good-mannered. They probably do say thank you afterwards. Wildly sentimental, they will remember birthdays, anniversaries, special days – and will sulk if you forget.

Libra Get On With

People of breeding! And at a superficial level, almost any of the signs except the ones that don't wash! Although as an air sign Libra quite enjoys the communication links with Gemini and Aquarius, they don't inherently trust Gemini, and Aquarius is certainly too unconventional to go down well. Capricorn they gravitate towards because of its respectability, its place in society and its ability to accumulate the good things of life. Cancer is liked for the same reason, though it is a bit of a gritty mix.

Virgo they love because it has often the same quality of social niceness, a bit prissy but always thoughtful and usually well bred. Leo they look up to – nothing comes higher up the social ladder than a monarch! And Libra can cope with all that monstrous ego.

Taurus, over-physical Capricorn and Scorpio are a real problem to Libra – all that earthy, dark, primitive passion and wallowing around in the flesh and the pleasures thereof. Libra would rather not know, thank you very much.

Aries can be a touch coarse and crass, but if well-matured can fit Libra well enough. Sagittarius is fun, communicative and socially conscious – so generally thought to be good news. Pisces is almost as bad as Libra at taking its own stand – the combination could drift around for ever, never making up their respective minds about anything!

Libra as Children

Can be almost too good to be true initially. Always wanting to please, until parents want to push them into rebellion, just to see them making a stand on their own. Either that or they argue with every statement anyone in the family makes, just to be sure the alternative point is made.

But either way, it adds up to the same conclusion. What they do is a reaction to what others have done first. Despite that, if propelled, they are an active sign with initiative. But you will have to teach them the virtues of self-assertion.

They adore pretty clothes, pretty colours and will cost you a pretty penny, no matter what sex they are, because they always head for the most expensive items in the shop. They also adore sticky, creamy, cakes!

Expect Libra girls to get on with Papa, the boys to have a special link with Mum, and the antipathies to do the reverse. Don't blame yourself that you don't get on with the same sex Libra – it is just the way they are designed.

Libra as Wives

Will maintain and decorate an exquisitely beautiful home, full of colour, elegance and refinement. On social occasions she will do you proud – wonderful hostess, agreeable guest and will dress with taste and flair.

She will be able to communicate well on any topic which interests you, maybe a few besides, and is equally happy in all-masculine company with your friends as she is in mixed.

But a Libra woman is not instinctively happy just being a homemaker and wife. She needs mental stimulation and, to be brutally honest, someone else to do the grubbier, more mundane chores around the house.

Libra as Husbands

If you like your husbands sweet, home-loving and helpful, you are on to a winner with Libra. Ever thoughtful about your needs, your feminine moods, your fanciful whims, your Libra fella will really understand you. He's generally an excellent father because he has that softer side. Ultimately he may be quite bad for you, because he won't stand up to you. So you get spoilt, sometimes petulant. Often Libra men marry aggressive women to take the initiative for them! After a while, having someone who only ever wants what you want can get tedious.

Libra as Bosses
By and large, really lovely. They won't ride roughshod over your ego just to show their position. Bullying is too coarse and inelegant to their way of thinking. The offices will be attractively decorated, colourful, light and airy. No grubby hovels with unwashed paintwork and inadequate loos – not if Libra's reputation is linked with it. They will bring you boxes of strawberry tarts and real cream cakes if they have to work you late. May drive you to distraction by dithering over decisions, but you can't have everything.

Libra as Slaves
Obsequious to the point of nausea – grovelling Libra is just what every Royal household requires. Will completely submerge their personality in their job and your identity. 'Your whim is my command' is Libra's motto anyway. Underneath it all there is probably a deeply resentful human being, but Libras never like going below the surface, not even their own, so they probably never realize how unhappy they are as slaves.

Favourite Saying
'If you tell me what you want, dear, that's what I want.'

Libra and Money
Can be a tiny problem area. Libras need to keep up with the Joneses, if not the Windsors, and therefore have very expensive tastes. Huge extravagances drive bank

managers to distraction. Even Libra's most tactful billets-doux don't work after a while. Libras need money – not millions. But they need not to have too many economic pressures on them. Poverty is so vulgar!

Libra Towards the Millennium

The enormous emotional changes which shook your life to its foundations in the early 1990s continue until 1995. In the process you left behind much that needed to be relegated to the dustbin, which had no place in your future. Frequent home moves or upheavals kept you rather insecure but never bored. Love and a lighter social life do not come together really until after 1995 when you have a real chance to let your hair down, kick over the traces and generally liven up a little. 1995/96 are your years of destiny when the turning point is reached. Then you make the decisions of a lifetime. The final four years of the decade are heavier in tone, hard working, more successful. Close partners will prove to be loyal.

Margaret Thatcher
13 October 1925

Margaret Thatcher is a shining example of the clear-thinking, sophisticated, rather remote Ice Queen Libra lady. Very much her father's daughter, she thinks in an incisive 'masculine' way. At one level she is extremely diplomatic, a much-needed quality for moving up the political ladder, and at a detached level she is a good social mixer. Earlier in her career she was a barrister: Libra is the scales of Justice. So she does have all the classic Libra traits, including a loathing for the great lazy unwashed!

But she has a ruthlessness not common in Libras, stemming from strong aspects to Mars and Pluto in her chart, which have helped her to the supreme leadership position. Mars rules Aries and has all that sign's hot-tempered impulsiveness, that 'shoots from the hip' and often leaps before it looks. Pluto rules Scorpio and gives her that will-to-power. Social niceties tend to take a back seat when it comes to the brass tacks of getting her own way. She can also be dogmatic to the point of obsession. She is certain her views are the only true ones.

Her loyalty to her own vision stems from a close contact between her lofty Leo Moon and idealistic Neptune. She believes in the dream she has in her mind of what society can become, and truly believes what she says. She is sensitive to atmosphere, and has probably had some prophetic dreams through her life.

The face she puts on for the outside world is a Saturn in Scorpio one, since that was on the horizon when she was born. She is skilled in business and finances, a great perfectionist and takes her responsibilities rather too seriously. This aspect she shares with the Queen. It makes both stern taskmasters, diligent and persistent.

She shares with J.F. Kennedy and the Duchess of Windsor a configuration in the chart known as a finger of destiny – fated changes of direction usually occur suddenly for these people. It produces people who have a dramatic impact on their society.

Margaret Thatcher's most successful period astrologically was 1979 to 1984 when Saturn was at the peak of her chart.

Luciano Pavarotti
12 October 1935

A massively complex but extremely lucky personality, the world's greatest tenor is probably unaware of the full extent of his talents or his good fortune. It comes relatively easily to him, so he regards it as unearned. He is both solidly practical and deeply emotional, but self-protective because he fears his sensitivities being hurt.

His Libra Sun makes him sweet, rather sentimental and very determined to be seen as someone with a bright, sharp mind. He takes great pride in his intellectual prowess. His life will always have been full of revolving crises which keep him constantly engaged in struggling to find a balance and to find peace. He needs space on his own at times to recentre himself, as too many people close to him make his nerves jangled.

A Leo Ascendant gives him an initial appearance of being rather overblown and boastful, but that quickly gives way to a more serene personality who likes to be kind. He was born in the mid-1930s at the time of a Saturn Neptune opposition which has produced many highly creative individuals, but he does veer at times into an almost frenzied state of anxiety about life. He is not always good at distinguishing between reality and unreality, and worries hugely about things which do not exist. His energy levels tend to rise and fall rather alarmingly, since he was a Full Moon baby.

Luckily, he is supported by a relaxed atmosphere at home, which he adores. He likes his own way but is willing to carry great responsibilities for his family. His emotional life is fairly sublimated for his career. He has never found relaxing, indulging or flirting very easy and prefers to be around a circle of acquaintances rather than intimate lovers.

He does have a strong sense of destiny with an emphasized Saturn Pluto trine. He knows he was put on earth for a significant purpose, which allows him to put up with the rigours of a tough career.

Michael Douglas
25 September 1944
Famous son of a famous father, Michael Douglas, son

of Kirk and star himself of *Wall Street* and *Fatal Attraction*, among others, is obviously driven by great fears of failure. His Libra Sun close to creative but rather vague Neptune is squaring Saturn. He gained the impression in childhood that he would only be loved if he achieved, and the standards he has set himself are so rigorously high that he is constantly putting himself down.

No matter how much money or praise his movies bring in, he will never be satisfied. He is prone to depression at times because he cannot relax and indulge himself as he sees other people doing. This strongly Saturnine influence is reminiscent of the late Richard Burton who, although a Scorpio, shared that same gloomy feeling about never really doing well enough, despite great career triumphs.

Neptune can also add a touch of confusion to his affairs. At times he worries too much that he is not liked, or imagines problems which later evaporate. All his enthusiasm for life, living and love appear to be directed towards his creative and inner life. He always puts duty first.

Michael Douglas's is a predominantly earth/air chart, which makes him practical and communicative. But he lacks a basic trust in life and a good connection to his feelings. He can be explosively over-emotional at times but typically he maintains a cool, rather detached approach. He copes best of all in a crowd of friends, surrounded by people who are not too intimate but give him affectionate support. With expansive Jupiter at the midheaven of his chart, he has earned himself a solid reputation in his career which can only develop as he grows older. He has that combination of luck and talent which seems to be a consistent thread through most successful personalities' charts.

CHAPTER 10

SUPERIOR SCORPIOS

IN A NUTSHELL
Power hungry, saints and sinners with an iron will.

Film
Bob Hoskins, Jaclyn Smith, Stefanie Powers, Burt Lancaster, Charles Bronson, Jeremy Brett, Sally Field, Nigel Havers, John Cleese, Bo Derek, Michael Jayston, Robert Hardy, Richard Burton, Grace Kelly, Vivien Leigh, Rock Hudson, Tatum O'Neal, Glynis Barber, Jodie Foster, Richard Dreyfuss, Goldie Hawn, Peter Cook, Julia Roberts.

Music
Bill Wyman, Simon Le Bon, Tim Rice, Lena Zavaroni, Art Garfunkel, Lulu, Cleo Laine, Petula Clark, Neil Young, Joni Mitchell, John Philip Sousa, Daniel Barenboim, Dame Joan Sutherland, Mahalia Jackson.

Sport
Lester Piggott, Diego Maradona, Gary Player, Frank Bruno, Nadia Comaneci, Willie Carson, Lucinda Green, Fulke Walwyn, Billie Jean King.

Politics
François Mitterrand, Indira Gandhi, Charles de Gaulle, Nehru, Theodore Roosevelt.

Royals
Prince Charles, King Hussein of Jordan, Shah of Iran.

Writers
Dick Francis, Margaret Mitchell, Hamish Hamilton, Dylan Thomas, Sylvia Plath, Robert Louis Stevenson, Albert Camus, George Eliot, Marghanita Laski, Ivan Turgenev, Dostoyevski, John Keats, R.B. Sheridan, Ezra Pound, Ionesco, Ronald Harwood, Donald Trelford, Nigel Dempster.

Art
Pablo Picasso, Monet, Jacob Epstein, Rodin, Benvenuto Cellini, Dame Elisabeth Frink, Johann Strauss, Borodin, Bizet, Paganini, Bellini.

The Good
St Augustine, Billy Graham.

The Infamous
Charles Manson, Joseph Goebbels, Tiberius.

Power figures, hugely determined sporting personalities, sex symbols, artists of note, investigators, and the odd black twisted soul. Scorpio does not believe in living life on the surface! Intensity is a character trait shared by all Scorpios, famous or not.

Lester Piggott, Billie Jean King, Nadia Comaneci have all succeeded because of that one trait shared by every Scorpio – obsessive, fanatical, sheer bloody-minded determination. Scorpios never listen when told they can't do something. They know they can do the impossible!

Scorpios don't care so much about the limelight as the power and influence the position brings, and their subsequent ability to control events. The heads of state and supreme political leaders like de Gaulle and Indira Gandhi were well-designed to handle the ultimate authority. They knew how to manipulate, were keen strategists and always formidable opponents.

A surprising number of eminent journalists and communicators appear in Scorpio's ranks. The newspaper editors amongst them share the political leaders' love of power but it is probably more a testament to Scorpio's deeply investigative nature. It loves getting to the bottom of other people's secrets. No surprise, therefore, to see Nigel Dempster here, who made a career out of ripping down the veils on top drawer private lives.

Always charismatic, Scorpios usually carry an air of brooding sexuality. They normally are not scared to throw themselves into the depths of their passions and indulgences. Hence Richard Burton. As artists they carry weight, substance, and not a little gloom. The dark side of Scorpio saw some meet rather tragic ends – like Sylvia Plath, Grace Kelly, Rock Hudson, the Shah of Iran. Good and evil are more inextricably mixed in Scorpio than any other sign, though Taurus, Gemini and Capricorn run it close! St Augustine and Billy Graham attempt to live only the good side; Tiberius, Charles Manson, Goebbels live the bad. Most Scorpios intuitively understand that you can't separate one from the other.

Scorpio in Essence

Deep, dark, determined, hugely resourceful, and in the right circumstances, a veritable miracle maker. Scorpio loathes living life on the surface, wants to get right down there into the murk if necessary to get the answers and the source of the power. Every sign, they say, fears or dislikes the one before. Scorpio regards Libra's light, superficial, let's-all-be-good-pals act with scathing contempt. This is not where life is at.

Although supremely good at uncovering other people's secrets, and getting to the bottom of mysteries, Scorpios regard their own secrets as sacrosanct. They are a very private sign, and will speak only when they feel it suits their purpose to do so – though they can be provoked into speech if you tramp on one of their corns. Revenge for slights uncoils the Scorpion's stinging tail faster than anything else.

They can, it has to be admitted, be a bit broody. They have elephant's memories for hurts done to them. Years go by, but the little black filing cabinet drawer keeps its record. One day, when opportunity presents itself – the pent-up vindictiveness has its moment. The hurt is avenged and Scorpio's sense of grievance is put to rest. Until the next time!

Being a Water sign, and a fixed one at that, Scorpio are very, very emotional even if the fairly controlled surface appearance suggests otherwise. Home and family are often weak spots of great sentimentality; the one place where the killer instinct is left behind, the over-controlled guard dropped.

Scorpios need an emotional life with guts and vitality. They do not appreciate wishy-washy partners. Frequently, Scorpios attract other Scorpios for that reason, though the power struggles that develop can be awful to behold. Jealousy and possessiveness are strong traits. The passions can get very primitive when their depths are tapped.

Scorpios often have an uncanny telepathy about other people's thoughts, and are also intrigued by other paranormal happenings. Fate and death fascinate them. They are highly unconventional, caring little for

121

the taboos of society. What is forbidden is precisely what will attract Scorpio. Life after death, spiritualism, reincarnation – the possibility of these is not frightening to them.

They need to know what lies beyond or below the surface reality of life. They strive always for the ultimate explanations, to rip aside the veils of convention or fear, and they do have the courage to step out into the blackness beyond. They are amongst the bravest of people.

They frequently have riveting eyes with a penetrating gaze which helps them to hold power over their audience. The eyes can captivate, seduce, flash with impatience, paralyse others with fear, and grow coldly blank if a sulk is descending. Scorpios can sulk longer, louder, blacker than you would believe possible if they have been thwarted. They cannot stand being manipulated. If someone else holds the power and they are forced to submit, the acid atmosphere that results is frightening.

Power, which is Scorpio's main motivation in life, causes them to be both viciously destructive and constructive. They destroy what is, so that they can build up what they want instead. In its negative form, this is mere manipulation – treating life and other people as a lump of plasticine to be remoulded to order. At its best, however, it is highly regenerative energy. Scorpio removes the obstacles to new growth, rather like the winter phase of nature. New life sprouts on the far side. Scorpios are at their best in situations of crisis – which are usually points of change. Out of catastrophe comes new life. The phoenix arises from the ashes.

Positive Traits
Are purposeful, powerful, highly imaginative, discerning, subtle, persistent, determined, never shallow,

penetrating, have incredible discipline, can balance materialism and spirituality, are investigative, can tune into others, are passionate, vital, gutsy, magnetic, charismatic, highly unconventional, will break taboos, are proud, sensitive, courageous in the extreme, loyal.

Negative Traits

Are jealous, resentful, stubborn, intractable, secretive and suspicious, caustic, sharp-tongued, wilful, obsessive, destructive, possessive, over-intense, explosive, impatient, bitter, sulky, self-satisfied, sexually arrogant, nurse grudges, are manipulative, power-hungry megalomaniacs.

Scorpio's Winning Streak

Scorpios never tell secrets. That can be irritating, but in highly confidential jobs it is a godsend. Scorpio friends attract more confidences than any other. Their discretion is very reassuring. Stamina, endurance, courage – Scorpio's obsessive traits come in very handy for long-distance projects. Nothing, but nothing, will deflect a Scorpio from a goal that has been firmly fixed. That bitter, sulky side has its plus points. Scorpios don't really care whether other people like them or not, so they won't shift ground just to gain approval. They do have more integrity than Libra, and can stand their ground no matter what the adverse reactions. That stinging tongue which causes so much offence also has its place. Often it is the hurtful comment which gets below the surface to the truth, that really hits home, which if listened to, does prompt change.

Scorpio as Lovers

Absolutely custom-built. Scorpio is always billed as the sexual sign *par excellence*. That isn't exclusively so – Taurus has a feel for the physical which is unrivalled.

But Scorpio can take sexuality into dimensions beyond the physical that Taurus never dreamt of. Scorpio is where the flesh and the spirit meet!

So if you like your love hot, passionate, vital, experimental, terribly intense, then Scorpio is your animal. But expect the emotions to operate at a level where love can easily flip over into hate. It is all or nothing, do or die. And if you decide to ditch them, there will be no forgiveness – not ever!

The pluses are sensitivity, commitment, lack of guilt, lack of self-consciousness. The minuses are over-whelming jealousy, sometimes overweening pride in their prowess, and an instinctive need to manipulate – all the time.

Scorpio Get On With

Curiously enough, other Scorpios. More marry within the sign than you would imagine. Probably because the other signs grow weary of all that intensity!

Scorpio adores emotion, so Cancer comes high on the list, though better Scorpio men with Cancer women. Scorpio ladies would eat Cancer men alive! Pisces are a touch wishy-washy, Libras certainly too milksop, and Sagittarians wouldn't stay around to be caught by all that dark energy!

Virgo and Gemini, if they are sufficiently full-blooded, have enough of a whiff of life, and the underworld, to descend to Scorpio's depths, though how long it would last is questionable.

The stronger Fire signs of Aries and Leo have the guts and vitality to earn Scorpio's respect, but fire and water don't tend to mix. The Fire signs disappear if they feel over-watered. They fear that Scorpio could quench their spirit for ever.

Aquarius is a terrible mix – all airy, detached and stubborn. Nothing that Scorpio likes there. At a pinch

Taurus might make a match – though depending on the personalities, it could make a murder as well.

Scorpio as Children

Have pity on yourself, parent. They can be the most difficult of children. Certainly they have the most to offer, but their black side is vile. Sulky, secretive with razor-sharp ripostes immediately to hand from two years onwards if you presume to push them in directions against their will.

They need to stretch to their limits in all directions, they need to plunge to the depths of everything. That's why they make the greatest saints and sinners. They have to plunge to the heart of the matter.

If you are of a lighter disposition, their need for intensity and challenge in relationships can be wearing. They are manipulative to a degree which will arouse anger you never knew you possessed.

First – find them another little Scorpio friend, and build them a secret hidey hole. That will give you hours of peace! Then give them things to make better. Anything broken down will do – equipment, furniture, sick animals. They aren't necessarily wonderful animal nurses, but they are great healers, and great restorers.

Lastly, learn to live with their murkier inclinations. They know by instinct that if they roll in the gutter long enough they will find a gold nugget. Final hint – grow a rhino skin. Scorpio children can be quite vicious to parents.

Scorpio as Wives

Scorpio women are usually good on the home front, and softer, more sentimental about home and family than their tough exterior suggests. But don't expect a meek, submissive mouse for a mate. Life will be a constant search for intensely meaningful moments.

Depending on your personalities, it may be a constant power struggle. 'You won the last round so I have to win this one'. Or 'I'll sulk forever if you don't let me win'. It can beat fainter hearts straight into the ground, where Scorpio's baser tendencies can tramp all over them.

You need a fairly stalwart personality and a few devious strategies up your sleeve to make life livable. But as with all things Scorpionic, the cost may be high, but the rewards are as well. Just don't expect to get away without paying! You need courage, in double doses.

Scorpio as Husbands

As above, but more so. Social conditioning about male superiority, added onto Scorpio's innate belief in their top dog status, can make Scorpio as a husband tricky. Or at least it means you will have a long and bloody training process to break him away from his megalomaniac leanings. Trouble is, they can be devilishly subtle strategists. They won't be brash about getting their own way. They just manipulate – all the time!

If you get a relatively mature, secure Scorpio they can be superb husbands – passionate and loyal, fond of family life, interesting and stimulating. But you will have to like long, brooding silences, and an obsessive need for their own privacy and secret spaces.

Scorpio as Bosses

Awful. They know every trick in the book about holding the reins of power and keeping control. They know every time you are up to no good, and tell you so smugly. In return they will divulge so little information to you that you have no elbow room for manoeuvre. Which is precisely the point – it keeps you dependent. Remember the old saying: 'Knowledge is power. Knowledge shared is power lost.' They won't share either. If you can stand total paternalism, they are just bearable.

Scorpio as Slaves
On the surface, excellent. Will grovel with the best of them. But beware! That hooded, oily smile hides a treacherous heart. They will plot and plan for years to overthrow you and grab power themselves. Submission breeds a terrible sense of resentment. They will subtly undermine your confidence, your position and your reputation. They will stir up trouble, foster mutiny, not always with themselves in the front line. They like mixing it – using other more gullible souls as ammunition.

Favourite Saying
'No comment.'

Scorpio and Money
One of Scorpio's strong points is handling money, especially in business. Although often extravagant at a personal level, Scorpios usually have a streak of common sense about cash. They do like security and will save for the future, though they can be wildly indulgent where the family is concerned.

Scorpio Towards the Millennium
The grinding down of your personality is never a totally pleasant process, but by the mid 1990s, looking back, it was perfectly obvious that the massive personal and emotional changes which had taken place since the late 1980s had been all worth the aggravation. You were going through a time of rebirth. The final half of the decade is the time to put all the positive results into action. Making money is now your aim in a fairly major

way. Changes at home speed up from 1995 onwards, with home moves and family upheavals being the order of the day until after 2000. The life's decisions you took in 1994 are now fully operational. Hard work is unavoidable, and health needs care in the final four years of the decade, but you are obviously on track for a productive time.

Prince Charles
14 November 1948

A deeply emotional man, much attached to home, highly sensitive and highly defensive, with a remarkable depth of insight into life's ultimate meanings. That is the main thrust of Prince Charles' birth chart.

As a Scorpio, of course, he is well adapted to power, influence and confidential matters. He has courage, resourcefulness, stamina and close emotional links to his family. His Sun was in the lower quadrant when he was born in the late evening: this suggests a deep commitment to his roots, his heritage, his family tree and indeed nature. It is where some of his more mystical bonds with the earth come from.

With Mercury in Scorpio, he is fascinated by the ultimate answers to life's questions, a trait doubled up by Pluto in his house of personality. There is a feeling from this that his entry into the world was a frightening one. From very early on he learnt to turn inwards to find his own personal sense of meaning.

His insights are penetrating, intuitive and accurate, but his tongue can grow a little caustic with that Mercury in Scorpio. Emotionally, he is incredibly idealistic – a natural-born romantic at heart. He really did want a Fairy Princess to marry. What he doesn't find easy are the more mundane aspects of everyday married life.

His fondness for children and great love of sport, especially of the equine variety, show up in the Mars Jupiter conjunction in Sagittarius. His wholehearted enthusiasms for these are a much-needed source of relaxation and nourishment from the pressures of a fairly ill-defined role. Scorpio likes to know where it is, and preferably likes to be in the number one slot. He is a great crusader. That Mars Jupiter aspect also appeared in J.F. Kennedy's chart, and they both share an enthusiasm for helping the less fortunate.

With the Moon in the tenth he was obviously close to his mother, and this positioning of the Moon suits him for a place of prominence in the public eye. He is incredibly sensitive to public moods and tastes, and will be an extremely popular figure in the years to come.

Goldie Hawn
21 November 1945

Bubbly, effervescent and frothy she may be on the surface, but Goldie Hawn is a true, stalwart Scorpio, with the determination of a battalion of Sherman tanks, when she sets her sights on a goal. She shares with Cher and Madonna a deep-seated fear of being controlled or dominated, so she makes extra sure that she is always in charge. Her tactics are often not straightforward or very obvious, but she can be a real volcano if thwarted.

Her sunny, solid reputation stems from an expansive Jupiter on the midheaven of her chart, giving every indication that her success will continue long past pension age. She always wanted to be creative, to be recognized for her artistic talents and also to scale the social ladder. But she also recognized early on that her tendency to be misunderstood could be turned to great advantage. With a hidden Mercury she feels she will not be heard clearly, and Neptune squaring her ascendant sets her up for wholesale confusion at times.

She adores being involved in team activities, being part of a group, and finds difficulty in deciding how she wants to play really close relationships. She will always have to work hard to make intimate partnerships in her life work. Her jealousy can sometimes be a problem, and she constantly worries about being betrayed or let down.

Her early experiences were, like those of many show business notables, less than deliriously happy. This has given her the drive to succeed at all costs. She constantly feels she has given less than her best so must try harder next time. In this way, she is probably always working at full stretch.

Her health is a little fragile, and she needs to watch that emotional upsets do not unsettle her energy levels. She is obviously happiest, with Uranus in the sixth house, doing a job that allows her to be a total individual, unrestrained in any way in her expression of herself.

John Cleese
27 October 1939

Another enormously funny but rather tortured comedian has been sculpted out of Scorpio clay in the shape of the ex-Monty Python star of *A Fish Called Wanda*. John Cleese has a chart of formidable obstinacy and endurance. With three Scorpio planets aspecting a fixed Mars, Pluto and Uranus, he was always destined for a life full of tension and rather spectacular firework displays. He really wants to be known as an intellectual, but fears in a quite depressive way that he is always going to be a failure. However, very little can shift him off track when he has made up his mind. He loathes interference in any form and needs to be allowed to wander his own highly individualistic path.

With a Moon Saturn conjunction in the eighth house, he shuts out a great deal of emotional intimacy, making close relationships quite a strain for both sides. He fears allowing anyone to reach him at a deep level, which must annoy his Scorpio Sun and highly sensual Scorpio Venus.

With Virgo rising and a first house Neptune, he gives out curiously mixed signals on first meeting of being rather meticulous, fastidious and enormously vague. He exerts a highly seductive fascination in the flesh, which is not always so obvious on screen.

He enjoys being influential in group activities and can be quite controlling with friends and associates, which sometimes runs him into arguments, but his seventh house Jupiter usually smooths over the rough edges. He can be ultra-charming, relaxed and enthusiastic when in the mood, which keeps him popular.

His interest in psychology and psychotherapy stems from his highly fixed chart which tends to hold emotions in too much. The build-up of toxins and tension from that have to be cleared out at some point in life, usually by illuminating the root causes of his inability to let go.

He needs to develop detachment in life, which he lacks with little air in his chart, and more free-flowing emotion, since he also lacks water. Luckily, he has an abundance of fiery energy around which gives him bounce, confidence and vitality. Fire has trust in life and contributes to a fertile creative imagination.

CHAPTER 11

SAGITTARIUS AT THE SUMMIT

IN A NUTSHELL
Jokers, thinkers, travellers – and definitely OTT.

Film
Jane Fonda, Christopher Plummer, Lee Remick, Christopher Cazenove, Kirk Douglas, Don Johnson, Kenneth Branagh, Kiefer Sutherland.

Film Directors
Steven Spielberg, Walt Disney, Otto Preminger, Michael Bogdanov.

Music
Tina Turner, Frank Sinatra, Sammy Davis Jnr, Edith Piaf, Jimi Hendrix, Joan Armatrading, Donny Osmond, Gilbert O'Sullivan, Connie Francis, Andy Williams, Keith Richards, James Galway, Dame Alicia Markova, Sir Kenneth MacMillan, Maria Callas, Elizabeth Schwarzkopf, José Carreras.

Comedians
Bette Midler, Woody Allen, Richard Pryor, Billy Connolly, Pamela Stephenson.

Sport
Chris Evert, Imran Khan, Lee Trevino, Johnny Francome.

Politics
Sir Winston Churchill, Willy Brandt, Bob Hawke, Tip O'Neill, Gary Hart, Ed Koch, Sir Geoffrey Howe.

Writers
Laurens Van der Post, Alexander Solzhenitsyn, Bhagwan Shree Rajneesh, Anna Freud, Margaret Mead, Edna O'Brien, John Osborne, Jean Genet, Rainer Maria Rilke, William Blake, Thomas Carlyle, Jonathan Swift, Mark Twain, James Thurber, Flaubert.

Art
Toulouse-Lautrec, Edvard Munch, Beethoven, Sibelius, Berlioz, Donizetti.

Super Rich
Christina Onassis, Aga Khan, J. Paul Getty, Andrew Carnegie, Sir Hugh Fraser, Randolph Hearst, Lord Forte, Madame Marie Tussaud.

'Small is beautiful' was never written by a Sagittarian, that's for sure. They think so wide, so high, so ludicrously inflated that your mind bulges at the edges just contemplating their exploits.

Steven Spielberg would have to be one. Walt Disney didn't do badly either on the scale of his output. The richest people in the world are well represented here with Christina Onassis, J.P. Getty (the original), the present Aga Khan, philanthropist multimillionaire Andrew Carnegie. Whatever Sagittarians do, they do big.

Where jokes are concerned, they often end up well

over the top! Bette Midler, Pamela Stephenson, Billy Connolly, Richard Pryor. All wild, a bit way out. They are usually quite delightful people, because Sagittarius is not a malicious sign, but the jokes have a habit of getting well out of hand. They take off like hot air balloons with no ballast. Sagittarians are not well grounded, don't have much sense of reality and when their ideas and enthusiasms catch hold of them, whoosh – up they go. They don't stop to think of the practical consequences.

But they do have the luck of the devil. It was lucky for Britain that Churchill was at the helm during World War II – reading the history of the war now, you realize how close a shave it actually was. But, when in tight corners, Sagittarians have a knack of ignoring the reality, rising above it and, by sheer force of their optimism, winning out. Something always turns up to rescue them, even at the eleventh hour.

Great thinkers and even not-so-great armchair philosophers abound. Sagittarius is interested in society, in belief systems, in philosophy, and in its own peculiarly jokey way is a strong moralist. Sartre once dubbed Sagittarian Jean Genet, the French homosexual writer banned at one time for obscenity, as 'the great moralist of this century'.

Sagittarius in Essence

Fairly insubstantial, to be honest. Solid, rooted, down to earth or tangible this last of the Fire signs absolutely is *not*. Fired with ideas and enthusiasms, sailing along on the cloud tops, travelling the wide open spaces, thinking great thoughts – all of those things are much closer to the essence.

In standard astrological textbooks Sagittarius is connected to the number nine, and to long-distance travel, higher education, philosophy, religion, society and its organization, and publishing. So as an energy it is either up in the head or on the move. What it isn't is grounded in the emotions or in physical reality.

Probably the most cheerful, certainly the most optimistic of the signs, Sagittarius always look on the bright side of things. They can be maniacally, obsessively, teeth-gritted smilers. They loathe above anything else being pulled back into Scorpio's black pit of despair. Each sign fears the one before!

So Sagittarius will find the silver lining in the worst horror, and pull a piece of positive thinking out of the hat when everyone else is reaching for the Valium. Their sense of humour never fails them, though at times it can be stretched to desperation point.

Although they can be unrealistic to a ludicrous degree, they are curiously an extremely honest sign, next to Leo probably the most honest of the zodiac. But not subtle. Friends of Sagittarians, it is always remarked, need the hides of ancient rhinos. The truth is delivered instantly, and devastatingly bluntly. 'Brutal' is an understated description of what comes out: the mouth opens and the thoughts tumble out unhindered by any filtering system whatsoever. The watery emotional signs always consider the emotional impact of their words first, and the sensible earthy ones consider the practical results, but fire just lets fly. And Sagittarians seem to have more opinions to deliver than Aries or Leo, the other two Fire signs. It is not meant at all unkindly, but the undiluted truth can be overpowering.

They like to horse around, are indeed often horsy, or just generally sporting, and have boisterously high spirits. They often have a childishly naive quality, and really don't like settling down to mature adult life. Too dull, mundane, routine, full of everything they find most boring. They need heroic adventures. Look at the moviemakers – Spielberg and Disney, making an adult career out of their childhood fantasies.

Sagittarius do exaggerate, at times wildly, and often can't deliver what they promised. Not because they mean to deceive – it's just those enthusiasms taking over. They really mean what they say, when they say it. They just haven't got round to thinking out the practicalities of how they can actually do what is so vividly in their head. Often they can't, or at least their interest fades before the tedious job of turning idea into reality is completed. Leave that to Capricorn!

The concept is Sagittarius' strong point. The idea, the overall strategy, the Grand Master Plan. Leave the drones and the minions to get on with the boring bits, like trying to make the Grand Plan work! Sagittarius does not like detail, fine print, moderation, or anything that requires too much stamina. They are not long-distance runners if they have to pound mile after mile on the hard road; they can be very long-distance travellers if they can put their feet up and fly!

Their hearty, hail-fellow-well-met attitude to life does not always meet with universal approval. They do rather expect other people to do the hard work, can sometimes demand total indulgence for their whims, and have been known to involve others in hugely grandiose schemes with very shaky foundations.

Positive Traits
Are jovial, optimistic, versatile, open-minded, adaptable, freedom-loving, sincere, honest, frank, dependable, have good judgement, have a wonderful sense of humour, laugh a lot, are high-spirited, are spontaneous, animated, idealistic, stimulating, interested in self improvement, sexy if the moment is right.

Negative Traits

Are prone to exaggeration, extremist, tactless, restless, careless, blindly optimistic, irresponsible, capricious, hate detail, childish, have erratic sex drives, want to impress, lecture you on your faults, narrow-minded, impersonal, immodest, are overambitious, have delusions of grandeur, are reckless gamblers.

Sagittarius' Winning Streak

You don't need me to tell you! It comes naturally to you to capitalize on your positive traits and completely ignore the not-so-wonderful bits.

But really you need to let your ideas, your enthusiasm and your confidence rip. Always keep your options open. Don't get tied down. Keep on the move and always look to the far horizon. Others don't have your breadth of vision, your scope, your ability to get miles above a situation and therefore see it in perspective. You never get too close to it to see clearly, as Virgo sometimes does.

Use that facility for honesty and straight speaking. It is a godsend in situations where insincere flattery and deceit have muddied the water. A strong, clear, courageous opinion cuts through yards of mush.

Finally, remember that jokers and court jesters have always played a hugely significant role. The jester was the only one who dared to tell the King the truth. He could do it because he wrapped it up in comedy.

Sagittarius as Lovers

All the Fire signs have a strong sex drive and are enthusiastic about passion. But Sagittarius in line with its restless, adaptable, never-stay-too-long-in-one-place energy, can be a touch erratic in the lovers' stakes. When they are there and their enthusiasm is on stream – wow. But their interest can wander on to other tracks fairly quickly.

They won't two time, generally, because they hate lying, and would much rather be straightforward. So you can expect to be told the truth – which won't always be to your liking or be too subtle/sensitive or tactful. But you will know where you stand.

Passionate and sexy they may be, but terribly physical they are not. It may sound a contradiction in terms, but they manage it! They're not turned on by anything too gross or too crude. Fantasy does turn them on, however, and most importantly fun. They need to laugh with love, and be good pals with lovers.

Sagittarius Get On With

Virtually everybody, initially, and even secondarily. Since they are an adaptable sign they can fit in, if pushed, with most temperaments. By choice they like fun, movement, chat – so Gemini suits them (as long as it is a bright, not dark Gemini). They also like Fire, so Aries and Leo fit. With Aries it could be so restless a mix they burn themselves out; Leo is better, and Sag can laugh at Leo's ego. Virgo also fits their needs for intelligent patter; is slightly lacking on the fun side but fills in for Sag's practical inadequacies.

Capricorn is a touch too serious, practical, and over-critical for sunny Sagittarius; and Taurus is a huge mismatch. Everything that Sagittarius is not, Taurus is – solid, rooted, earthy, stubborn, enduring. Opposites may attract initially, but a complete lack of common points of contact soon chills the atmosphere.

The water signs make Sagittarius uneasy. Pisces is the best of a difficult bunch for them. But Cancer curtails their freedom, and Scorpio bodes gloom.

The Air signs can often work well with all Sagittarius's fiery ideas. Gemini is top of the list, Aquarius next, though it might end up a fairly detached attachment, and Libra's light, keep-it-bright-on-the-surface attitude to life accords well with their own inclinations.

Sagittarius as Children

Excruciatingly happy little souls on the whole, unless something is very wrong in the atmosphere. They live in their daydreams, play out amazing adventure fantasies, and hate doing all the tasks you try to set them. They do have to learn a modicum of sense about the benefits of discipline and long-term effort, but it is doubtful if childhood will teach them it – leave it to life.

Their unfailing optimism will give cheer to the more doom-laden members of the family. They'll always be full of bright thoughts of comfort for your crises. Let them read endlessly – anything in the historical, social, philosophical, even religious line. Send them sporting. They don't like the cold and the rain but they do like exercise.

Stop worrying about them! Life is kinder, with less justification, to lazy, sloppy, undeserving Sagittarians than anyone else. They'll do very nicely, thank you, most of the time.

Sagittarius as Wives

This is not at all a domestic sign. Doesn't like being tied down, hates routine chores, isn't interested in dirt and the removal thereof. Would much rather be wrapped up in an armchair with a good book or preferably travelling round the world. Chris Evert is a fairly typical lady. Her interests lie well outside the home and family realm. Jane Fonda certainly has a family, but how much can she possibly see of them with all her other interests? It needs to be a fairly unconventional setup to suit Sagittarian wives – with bags of freedom, stimulation and fun.

Sagittarius as Husbands

Sweet, charming, full of fun, tend not to grow up until well into the latter stages of life, tend to be irresponsible, impractical, and will go flying into wildly grandiose schemes that come unstuck! You need to be very down-to-earth to cope with the extreme end of Sagittarius as a husband. The more middle-of-the-road variety have the above toned down to more reasonable proportions.

But don't expect a handyman about the house, or a father who will lay down and follow up long-running disciplinary projects.

A moral authority he may be, and he'll lay down the law about the theory of behaviour. Just don't expect him to make the practice stick. But he will be honest, straightforward and really does not like deceiving, so he's a better bet than quite a few signs.

Sagittarius as Bosses

If you like doing all the work, his/hers as well as yours, they can be charming to work for. Never a sour or cross word, unfailing optimism when you think the entire office is about to collapse, always ready for an afternoon's innocent fun. What more could you ask for? On the down side, they will not settle to paperwork or make decisions about boring practical necessities of life. That's all your job.

They will offer you pay rises they can't possibly afford on the cash flow, so you'll have to refuse – painful, that! They will ultimately get a little boring about the millions the firm is about to make . . . sometime in the future, very soon. Unless, of course, you happen to be working for Steven Spielberg.

Sagittarius as Slaves

Not bad, though a bit blunt at times. Adaptable,

friendly, won't sulk and will always be assuming life has to get better, so it doesn't matter if the present is a disaster. They will be so determinedly looking on the bright side of things that they probably won't notice their position as slave anyway.

Favourite Saying
'I've got this absolutely wonderful scheme – it can't fail.'

Sagittarius and Money
Usually very bad news indeed. Money is their absolute Achilles' heel. They are reckless, overoptimistic, and gamblers by instinct even if they never go near the horses or the tables. They take risks that turn the bank manager's hair grey once the reality beneath all those bright ideas actually sinks in.

Having said all that, they are also extremely lucky and all that charm is good at extracting money out of banks, and blood from stones. But really they need reliable financial partners who will handle all the practical details.

Sagittarius Towards the Millennium
Finances, which were on a real roller-coaster ride for the first half of the 1990s, stabilize mid-way through. Psychological changes ongoing since the mid 1980s change gear in 1995, as Pluto moves into Sagittarius. Now comes the real growth – of a new identity, a whole new way of living. Sunny good fortune in substantial quantity is yours in 1995. But rebirths do not come without a struggle. Until the turn of the century you are wrestling with deep, often anguished questions about who you are. Life is not all profound, however. Speedy influences have you racing around at high speed at the same time. Everyday existence will be a constant

variety of events. Nothing will stay the same for long.

Jane Fonda
21 December 1937

An exceedingly complex chart matches Jane Fonda's exceedingly complex personality. No two-dimensional celluloid goddess is she. With Sun and Venus in Sagittarius in the chart area ruling entertainment, children and love affairs, all of these have played a significant role in her life. Her ascendant sign is Leo, doubling up on that sunny, colourful, extroverted personality that wants to be noticed. Everything she does is on the grand scale.

Her relationship with her parents is stressed in the chart, and indicates a level of unhappiness below the surface glitter. With Uranus at the peak of the sky when she was born, she would have a mother who was unpredictable. It has turned her into a highly individualistic personality, who will go her own way, no matter what the reaction. Look at the hostility she attracted over her stand on Vietnam: it was easier that way for her than fitting in with the consensus view. She does not see herself as a conventional person.

She is driven by a tremendous quantity of anger and guilt. Her father, whom she adored but felt separate from most of her life, put such a level of expectation into her head that she has always felt a failure. She never felt she matched up to what was expected. Even now she will not feel satisfied with her efforts. She finds relaxation extraordinarily difficult.

She will be energetic around the house. Slouchers won't be given an easy ride. With the Moon in Leo, she likes being the centre of attention, and also more drawn to the grand style of life than some of her left-wing views may suggest.

An immensely complex character, she has a

multitude of talents and a real sense of mission about her life. She is tuned into public taste and can therefore pick up on popular trends before they appear. It does mean she changes frequently in her outlook and beliefs. It is an ability not so much to drift with the tide, but to move before the tide has started to surge. In this way, she looks as if she created aerobics, for example; in fact, she merely sensed it was the coming thing.

Steven Spielberg
18 December 1946

How does he do it? Why does he do it? These are the two questions all of Hollywood wants answered about the endlessly successful billionaire.

The 'why' is probably for himself. He has a lower hemisphere chart. With one exception, all the planets were below the horizon when he was born. So he sees life very much from his own perspective. Me – I'm in the middle, and any view of life starts with how it affects me.

He also has the Saturn Pluto conjunction in his house of money. In some astrological textbooks, this is described as the aspect of the magician. It is a truly formidable energy and can be destructive – hence the violence of some of the movies – as well as constructive. But he certainly will have a strong sense of the value of money and an even stronger compulsion to control it for himself. All of that overshadows Sagittarius' total blank spot about cash.

His Sagittarius Sun, full of zip and ideas, is in the area of hard work, close to acquisitive Mars in Capricorn, and opposite Uranus which suits him well for an unpredictable business. He thrives on excitement, high adrenalin flow and being able to do his own thing.

With Moon, Jupiter and Venus in Scorpio he is shy about his emotions, although he can be kind and generous. He must have spent much of his childhood lost in daydream, and the fantasies into which he escaped then have provided him with the ideas for his movies. The films he makes today are packed with the fun he wished he had. Early on he learned to create non-humans whom he could relate to in safety, and he later capitalized on this with the popular film *E.T.*

He is fascinated by the paranormal, the occult, maybe even astrology. Part of this stems from the magical strain in his chart, part of it from Scorpio which loves to delve into the hidden depths, and part of it from Uranus in the hidden twelfth house of his chart. Although he is afraid of being different from others, he is in fact unique. Once he accepts this and his special interest in the paranormal, the tension recedes. His home and emotional life will never be as easy for him as his working life. Careerwise, he is not really into his proper stride yet, despite the billions. The best will come after his mid-forties.

Tina Turner
25 November 1941

The rock'n'roll star's chart oozes life, vitality and energy. Her fiery Sagittarius Sun is magnificently aspected by an Aries Mars and Pluto in Leo creating a grand triangle of fire in the chart.

She is spontaneous, impulsive, naturally adventurous and has an unshakeable belief in herself. A streak of naturally appealing innocence allows her to take enormous risks. She aims straight for excitement with little fear, insecurity or restraint.

Her much-publicized problems with a domineering, and at times brutal, ex-husband really stem from a difficult childhood. Her Sun in Sagittarius was sitting almost exactly opposite Saturn and Uranus at the end of Taurus. She learned very early on that life was a struggle, that nothing much came easily. Happily, Saturn mellows with the years. She ultimately came to trust more in life and broke free from the shackles of a destructive marriage. Now her fire energies can be let loose in all their colour, ferocity and warmth.

Saturn makes early life a misery, but the benefits came late on. Usually a chart with strongly Saturnine influences indicates a life that is lived upside down. She would be an old, serious child. Now she is in a youthful – and how – middle age. She will never look her years from now on. Her childhood was chilly; the latter third of her life will be warm.

She will always live an unpredictable, exciting lifestyle. Anything too static would pall quickly. That Saturn Uranus contact does make her veer from extreme to extreme. One day quite cautious and traditional, the next day outrageously radical. With Mercury in Scorpio, she is never lost for an apt phrase.

Although with Mars aspecting Pluto her stage act projects an image of earthy uninhibited sensuality, in reality, off stage, she is quite reserved in public. She likes to look dignified and wealthy, and adores dining out in the best places.

CHAPTER 12

CAPRICORN CROWNS

IN A NUTSHELL
Arch achievers, heavyweights, sensualists and sadists.

Film
Mel Gibson, Anthony Hopkins, Faye Dunaway, Anthony Andrews, Maggie Smith, Victoria Principal, Sarah Miles, Jon Voight, Dyan Cannon, Rowan Atkinson, Linda Lovelace, Humphrey Bogart, Ava Gardner, Marlene Dietrich, Cary Grant, Jane Lapotaire, Jason Connery, Michael Crawford, Diane Keaton, Kirstie Alley, Kevin Costner.

Film Directors
Richard Lester, Ismail Merchant, Federico Fellini, J. Arthur Rank.

Music
Elvis Presley, Rod Stewart, David Bowie, Shirley Bassey, Dolly Parton, Jack Jones, John Denver, Joan Baez, Marianne Faithfull, Janis Joplin, Annie Lennox, Paul Young, Nigel Kennedy, Grace Bumbry.

Sport
Muhammad Ali, Joe Frazier, Floyd Patterson, Harvey Smith, Stefan Edberg.

Power Figures

Idi Amin, Stalin, Mao Tse Tung, J. Edgar Hoover, Al Capone, Ian Brady, Hermann Göring, Kim Philby, Howard Hughes.

Politics

P.W. Botha, Richard Nixon, Conrad Adenauer, Walter Mondale, Barry Goldwater, Clement Attlee, Benjamin Disraeli, David Lloyd George, Raisa Gorbachev.

Royals

Princess Alexandra, Princess Michael of Kent, Queen Silvia of Sweden, King Juan Carlos.

Writers

Henry Miller, Edgar Allan Poe, J.D. Salinger, E.M. Forster, Simon Raven, Gerald Durrell, J.R.R. Tolkien, Jacob Grimm, Rudyard Kipling.

Art

Matisse, Cézanne, Augustus John, Puccini.

Religious

Albert Schweitzer, Simon Wiesenthal, Louis Pasteur, Joan of Arc, St Ignatius Loyola, St Bernadette, Gurdjieff.

Capricorn personalities are no mean achievers. They set their sights high, then bend with a will into whatever sweat, discipline, and effort it takes to get them to the mountain top.

Heavyweight boxers are a good example at a physical level. Muhammad Ali, Joe Frazier, Floyd Patterson – world champions at the toughest endurance test. They suffer their way to status, money, respect. They don't want to win for winning's sake, like Aries, or for the ego boost, like Leo. They want the position, standing on the peak. Others must then look up to them.

Capricorn is good at acquiring money, through pain and tears if necessary, because of an ability to turn ideas into something tangible. It combines creativity with enormously practicality and a healthy streak of materialism. No surprise, therefore, to find some extremely wealthy names – Howard Hughes, Elvis Presley, and one of the world's wealthiest countries, Saudi Arabia.

Deeply attached to traditional values, it is also a snobbish sign. Most Capricorns, unless born into the upper echelons of society, are definitely socially ambitious: hence Princess Michael. Capricorns like being superior.

At the negative end, this trait has produced an unholy collection of dictators and sadists. Capricorn shares not only heavyweight boxers with Taurus, but brutal power as well. Just look at Idi Amin, Stalin, Mao Tse Tung, Moors murderer Ian Brady, Al Capone, P.W. Botha – all Capricorns – men who maintained their power and position by gross physical means. Too much of the earth element, and personalities lose touch with sensitivity, emotion and the ability to image the effects of their actions.

This negative overemphasis on the physical has also produced a strain of sensualist Capricorns, so into the indulgences of the flesh they damage themselves – like Presley, Janis Joplin, Marianne Faithfull.

Capricorn in Essence

The essential Capricorn is about solid, substantial achievement. As a practical, down-to-earth sign, it wants practical reasons for everything – and more importantly, a tangible result (preferably in money and possessions)!

As an active cardinal sign, Capricorn also has bags of initiative, resourcefulness and get-up-and-go. Early life is generally a real struggle, so the results of that energy will be slow in arriving. Most Capricorns either have poverty-stricken childhoods or chilly unemotional ones. They are old, serious children. Happily, they mellow with the years. The first third is generally difficult, the middle third is defrosting, the last third of life is everything the first third was not – warm, successful, richer.

And Capricorns have an obsession about saving up for the rainy days of their old age, as they see it. They talk more about their retirement cottages than anyone else! But really, it is a manic drive to make sure the end is better than the start.

As life gets easier on the way through, they also get younger looking! Capricorn children look like Rip Van Winkle and Capricorn geriatrics look like childish imps. The women don't wrinkle as fast as other signs in their middle years.

Overwork can be a real problem, and in early life so can a doubting, overserious approach to the task of living. Most Capricorns need to keep reminding themselves that a good laugh and a frivolous outing are allowed. Not everything in life needs to have a purpose or a goal. Capricorns tend to read books that are good for them, rather than just plain relaxing. They go to movies that have a meaning, or to first nights because it is good for the social image. Leisure that is solely fun is for lesser mortals.

Saturn, which rules Capricorn, is a controlling, defensive energy, so Capricorns usually put up a public face which is austere, maybe a touch formidable, a little distancing. Once through the outer barrier, however, a very different human being emerges – funny, highly sexual, full of life. But that inner face rarely appears in public or out on social occasions.

Capricorn hates the idea of ridicule almost as much

as Cancer, and will stand on its dignity with real determination. Neither sign finds it easy to stand back and laugh at themselves. And a betrayed Capricorn will extract horrible revenge for their sense of personal outrage. Saturn can be viciously vindictive – all the nastier because it can do it in a chilly, unemotional way.

Capricorn finds emotion a problem, certainly won't display affection in public, and even in private can find verbalizing what it feels tricky. Sadly, many Capricorns are so anxious about material security that they marry for it. Then stick out chilly marriages for years because their excessive concern for social status won't let them admit publicly to having failed. This is a dreadful shame, because all that sensual, earthy passion then lies unused.

They can be lonely people because of the emotional reserve, but that then suits them well for the executive positions in life to which they often aspire. If the barriers don't come down as they ought, at least in private, they can end up very isolated – like Howard Hughes, and Elvis Presley, suspicious, distrustful, completely cut off.

Home can be a noisy area; children a source of great satisfaction. Friends are usually powerful and aggressive, spouses supportive, money erratic but well under personal control. Time spent in private is devoted to thinking deep thoughts about the world and reading philosophical books.

Positive Traits

Reliable, determined, ambitious, careful, prudent, have a sense of humour and a sense of discipline, have integrity, are patient, persevering, kind, earthy, basic, sensible, duty conscious, efficient, sensual, passionate, intuitive, steady, surefooted, neat, methodical, are good troubleshooters, are sensitive.

Negative Traits
Rigid in outlook, overexacting, pessimistic, scrooges, too conventional, mean, miserly, wet blankets, insensitive, self-important, cynical, cold, have a false sense of themselves as martyrs, are manipulative, pretentious, snobs, can't share or cooperate, have no sense of humour, are celibate.

Capricorn's Winning Streak
Capricorn stands on the threshold between the realm of ideas and the realm of the real world. Your great strength is the ability to turn those ideas into tangible reality. Pisces has great ideas, Sagittarius has great plans – but both lack the ability or the will to do anything about them, so the ideas stay up in the air. You have practical common sense, great ambition and the capacity to work till you achieve your goals. Your self-sufficiency, which sometimes cuts you off from relationships, is a great help to you in terms of your life goals. If success is truly one part inspiration to nine parts determination, you have the 100 per cent taped.

   Your conventional attitude to life, which other more radical souls castigate as stuffy, is what holds society together. You create the wealth and uphold the solid, middle-of-the-road values which give stability. You know that laying the foundations is the vital part of the building process, so you are willing to labour long and hard at the unseen, unglamorous tasks to make sure the end result will stand the test of time.

Capricorn as Lovers
It depends whether they have found their way behind their defences, or not. They need commitment before they will let their barriers down; and can be so obsessed with wanting to know the right way of doing it, you feel as if you were making love to a rule book. 'Is this how

151

the best people do it?' You can't let the passions rip with that amount of self-consciousness about.

Capricorns can remain celibate for years, or stay with partners whom they are not sexually attracted to – and then they fall through the trapdoor! Once they have broken down their barriers they can be very sexually active, highly sensual, as befits a true Earth sign, passionate and funny. Their two sides are as chalk to cheese. But they need deep love and one day, with luck, most of them find it.

Capricorn Get On With

People of breeding and position – so Libra fit well and won't embarrass them in public, which is a prime requirement. The other two earth signs, Virgo and Taurus, are respected for their practical, hard-working streak. But Virgo is preferred because of its genteel side. Taurus can be a little coarse, and playful in public.

Leo should be a good mix since it has all the regal, rich trappings, but somehow appears too flash, too vulgar and a touch empty to Capricorn. Glitter is not Capricorn's thing at all, and Leo showing off in public is too flesh-crawlingly embarrassing for words. Aries equally is a public spectacle – all that spontaneous impulsiveness attracts quite a few egg yolks dripping down lapels. Aries couldn't care less, but Capricorn dies a million deaths. Sagittarius is almost bearable if very negative, therefore narrow-minded, highly traditional. But happy-go-lucky bigmouth Sag is a definite non-starter.

Some Geminis suit, as long as their dark side is kept out of sight. Their light, unemotional touch doesn't pull Capricorn into its feelings too much. Aquarius is far too eccentric, anarchic and downright shocking – doesn't give a fig about convention. Initially Aquarius may seem OK, as it has a Saturnine face as well, but it won't last. Scorpio is far too murky in inclination to suit any but the over-physical Capricorns. Pisces can suit, if weak, because it follows meekly behind; and if highly successful, because it adds status to Capricorn's position. People who are highly successful in business are often either Capricorn or Pisces.

Capricorn as Children
Often have all the spontaneity, gaiety and warmth of Queen Victoria in her declining years. Overcautious, mistrustful, over-obedient, insistent about knowing the rules and regulations – and sticking to them. Happily, that mellows later in life. But they do have an aversion to playing and relaxing. Try to make them laugh! Give, and give and give emotional warmth to them. Don't mistake their defensive barrier for rejection; you need to defrost that icy exterior before you find Capricorn junior's heart.

Don't worry too much about that ambitious, materialistic side. It will stand you in good stead later in life – Capricorns always have deep feelings of obligation and duty towards parents. So you'll be grateful for their capitalist abilities.

Capricorn as Wives
Will be dutiful, good on social occasions, the classier the better. Will bring the children up with proper sense of discipline and a proper set of morals. Will always understand if you have to work hideously long hours – they like the results of your labours. Can be exceptionally warm beneath the polite surface. But they can also marry for money, and stick out a refrigerated marriage for the sake of status, for longer than you would believe possible.

Capricorn as Husbands
Excellent breadwinners, they are conscientious, dutiful,

loyal, hard-working, and like to be active around the house. They can be useful at a practical level as handymen as long as they haven't risen too high in their sense of self-importance – but then they will probably be rich enough to pay somebody to do the job.

Early marriages will tend to be very detached affairs; later Capricorn marriages stand more of a chance of sparkle and life.

In the fidelity stakes, Capricorn is honourable but odd. Will protect your public reputation at all costs, so affairs are likely to be secret. But their taste in mistresses can be extremely bizarre: so far removed from their spouses, it is laughable. A touch of the old Victorian – wives, mothers and sisters get respect, kitchen wenches are where the fun is.

Capricorn as Bosses

Custom built. Capricorn is the stuff on which capitalism is founded. The boss will be distant, conscious of his or her position, boringly punctual. Will probably arrive first in the morning, anytime from 6.30 am onwards, and therefore notice as you slouch in at 9.45. Will insist on short hair, women wearing skirts, and no ostentatious jewellery. And no swearing! Will deliver lectures on the evils of laziness. Will work hideously late in the evening and therefore notice as you nip out at 4.45 pm.

Although quite paternalistic, will take the responsibilities of being boss very seriously. So the plus side includes very fair treatment, rewards (not excessive) for hard work and productivity, and frequent (though moderate) compliments on your efforts.

Capricorn as Slaves

Will act as meek as lambs while it suits the long-term purpose. Very good at carrying out orders. Discipline and obedience are what they thrive on, no matter which side of the orders they are on. Then one day – suddenly – as the boss disappears, they step into his place. Other slaves be warned: be nice to Capricorns, no matter how lowly. They always move up.

Favourite Saying
'You can't do that – people might see!' 'I'm sure the Queen doesn't do it that way.'

Capricorns and Money
In the long term, excellent. Though curiously, Capricorns tend to earn their money in unusual ways and have fairly erratic bank balances. Much thought goes into the handling and development of joint finances, so either household budgets or business money are an area in which Capricorn's talent shines. They can be stingy as well, but they can also be extravagant. If you want to emulate the highest in the land, it doesn't come cheap.

Capricorn Towards the Millennium
The shake-up which the late 1980s and early 1990s provided for you has repercussions well past the turn of the century. Your life was turned inside out and upside down, but the end result was a sense of being a totally different person. The 1991/1992 Eclipses also did their piece in reorganizing your relationships and your life's direction. The rest of the decade is spent in reassessing your values and trying to bring sense into a fairly erratic financial situation. By 1995, a long phase of psychological clearing out begins which can only have beneficial results. Life feels fortunate and favoured in 1996. Your domestic situation becomes firmer for the final four years of the decade. You may well have to face up to tensions, but the air will be cleared for new emotional beginnings.

Anthony Hopkins
31 December 1937

Anthony Hopkins' chart reflects his 'magical' gift for acting, but it also reflects the price he has had to pay for his genius – in loneliness, isolation, oversensitivity, deep insecurity and psychological pain. Happily, like most Capricorns he is finding that life becomes easier, mellower, warmer the older he gets.

The creative talent, the voice as an artistic instrument, the ability to make a vision into something tangible, all come from a concentration of Sun, Mercury and Venus in Capricorn in the sunniest area of his chart. He lives through acting.

Saturn sitting opposite Neptune gives him his almost unlimited access to those magical realms of non-reality where fantasy lives. It produces a fairly precarious balance for everyday living, but the mystical visions and glimpses of Dionysian madness it offers are inexhaustible sources of inspiration.

At first glance his is an awesome chart with a rich, multi-dimensional pattern of interconnected planets, confusing in its complexity. The elements are at war – sensitivity vies with dead weight; the imagination is limitless but the vision is narrow; there is a need for spirituality and a yearning for decadence; ruthless ambition and the urge to a total surrender of the ego; kindness and compassion coexist with black, violent anger.

The enormous benefits of his visionary potential with strongly aspected Neptune and Pisces don't come cheap. His need to merge with the spiritual, to get out of reality, led in his twenties and thirties to him drinking himself steadily towards oblivion. Happily, his chart carries a configuration known as a finger of destiny. It produced the sudden change of direction necessary to stop his self-destruction.

Not surprisingly, given his concentration of planets in Capricorn, he is attracted to playing dictators. He admits cheerfully to being a bit of a monster himself and to be fascinated by the self-obsessed megalo-maniacs of history . . . Lenin, Stalin, Hitler, and of course the fictitious newspaper baron Lambert Le Roux he plays with such bravado in 'Pravda'.

Then in the early 1990s he found a film role which so fitted the zeitgeist of the age that it became a Hollywood hit. His portrayal of the coldblooded psychopathic killer, Hannibal Lecter, gave him his first really solid success on the international scene. He is now on an upward curve careerwise which will go on and on. His very best is still in front of him: his sixties should be memorable.

Princess Michael
15 January 1945

Princess Michael's chart is a curious mixture of down-to-earth, practical, socially conscious Capricorn and an almost equally head-in-the-clouds Neptune.

With Mars in Capricorn, she is intensely ambitious for status and recognition. Her actions will be thought out and carefully calculated to achieve money and professional advancement.

She is capable of decisive action when her energy is effectively channelled. She will have all of Capricorn's conventional horror for laziness, lack of ambition and anything that smells like an irresponsible way of life. She desperately wants her children to amount to something.

Neptune, on the other hand, is emphasized in her chart, sitting on the point of a T square. She wants to think the best about people but is often disappointed. Once she gets hold of the positive end of that Neptune, she does have artistic, literary and communication talents which she can put to excellent use. She is also able to give comfort to others: Neptune is a highly compassionate energy.

Her early life, with Saturn in Cancer, was chilly and Mars in opposition to Saturn suggests an over-authoritarian, austere father. Her position in the public eye with Mars Neptune aspects has attracted difficult publicity to her since Neptune began to transit that T square in 1984.

Only when Uranus and Neptune have finally cleared her Capricorn Cancer planets after the mid 1990s will her life finally settle into a happier, more peaceful pattern. She is finding a softer, more feminine self and leaving the rather compulsive publicity seeking urges of her ego behind.

Mel Gibson
16 January 1956

Australia's lethal weapon and megastar sex symbol has the rough and ready, almost violent energies in his chart of which Mad Max himself would be proud. His ambitious Capricorn Sun opposing Uranus pushed him early into dreams of being different. His goals in life have always been fanatical, slightly off the wall, but he made them stick by sheer earthy determination. At times his obsessiveness can be downright perverse as he wilfully continues along his own path.

But with amiable Jupiter close to powerfully persuasive Pluto opposing his Moon and Venus, he can always be relied on to charm away any rough edges of people's irritation. He carries the Peter Pan image of Capricorn with a beguiling little-boy-lost look for women. His Moon Jupiter connection also allows him to be sugary sweet and sentimental when it suits him, though he can also be as hard as nails. Jupiter Pluto is always a little over the top in expansionist tendencies which may go a long way to explain his large family.

He is a real law unto himself from several different angles, and will do what he thinks fit, no matter what the resistance. He needs to be in control, to be the one who has the final say.

He is perfectly used to putting up with tough times, as he was brought up in an environment where his individual needs were not much catered for. He learnt to bite his tongue when necessary, though he then can explode noisily when it all gets too much for him.

With Mars and Saturn in Sagittarius close to the node, he was destined to carry the image of a ruthless, violently physical male for society. That rootless, uncommitted quality which fits him so well for those dashing film roles is one which he will slowly abandon as he ages. Ultimately, he may even come to represent a more educated type as he broadens his vision.

CHAPTER 13

AQUARIUS ADVANCE GUARD

IN A NUTSHELL
Shockers, sexperts, pioneers and rebels.

Film

Tom Selleck, Gene Hackman, Charlotte Rampling, George Segal, Alan Alda, Paul Newman, Robert Wagner, Telly Savalas, Burt Reynolds, Alan Bates, Zsa Zsa Gabor, Katherine Ross, Nastassia Kinski, Vanessa Redgrave, Mia Farrow, Farrah Fawcett, Tallulah Bankhead, Jack Lemmon, Oliver Reed, Morgan Fairchild, John Travolta, Carol Channing, Jean Simmons, Simon MacCorkindale, Janet Suzman, Lana Turner, Elaine Stritch, Prunella Gee, Jane Seymour, Greta Scacchi, Claire Bloom, Sinead Cusack, Cybill Shepherd, Martin Shaw, John Hurt, Humphrey Bogart, Clark Gable, John Forsythe, Ernest Borgnine, James Dean.

Film Directors

Franco Zeffirelli, John Schlesinger, Milos Forman, Roger Vadim, Joseph Mankiewicz, Alan Parker.

Music

Eartha Kitt, Andrew Ridgeley, Renata Tebaldi, Don

Everly, Neil Diamond, Nick Mason, Stan Getz, Gene Pitney, Holly Johnson, Stephane Grappelli, Jimmy Van Heusen, Yoko Ono, Carol King, Placido Domingo, Sir Geraint Evans, Jerome Kern, Acker Bilk, Mikhail Baryshnikov, John Ogdon, Alice Cooper, Jacqueline du Pré, Hal Prince, John Williams (film composer).

Comedians
Terry Jones, Shelley Berman, Ned Sherrin, Barry Humphries.

Sport
John McEnroe, Greg Norman, Jack Nicklaus, Mark Spitz, Jody Scheckter, Sandy Lyle, Paddy McMahon, John Surtees, Virginia Leng, Fred Trueman, Bernard Gallagher, Wayne Bretzky.

Politics
Dan Quayle, Ronald Reagan, Giscard d'Estaing, Yassar Arafat, Abba Eban, Lord Randolph Churchill, Abraham Lincoln, Franklin Roosevelt.

Royals
Princess Caroline of Monaco, Princess Stephanie of Monaco, Queen Beatrix of the Netherlands, Princess Marie Astrid of Luxembourg.

Writers
William Burroughs, Desmond Morris, Len Deighton, Germaine Greer, Betty Friedan, Helen Gurley Brown, James Joyce, Colette, Lord Byron, Robert Burns, Rabelais, Norman Mailer, Susan Hill, Virginia Woolf, Stendhal, Lewis Carroll, Somerset Maugham, Anton Chekhov, Muriel Spark, Charles Darwin, Havelock Ellis, Dr Alex Comfort, Charles Dickens, Boris Pasternak, Christopher Marlowe, Paul Hamlyn, August Strindberg, Bertolt Brecht.

Art
Edouard Manet, Franz Schubert, W.A. Mozart, Felix Mendelssohn.

Explorers
Freya Stark, Ernest Shackleton.

Unconventional, highly individualistic personalities – John McEnroe, Yoko Ono, Germaine Greer, Barry Humphries, Lord Byron. In their own, sometimes quite eccentric way, they just do their own thing. If the rest of the world is shocked, that's their problem. Aquarians don't really care. They came into the world feeling misunderstood, so being out of step with common opinion just feels natural.

Sex looms large if you skip down the lists – renowned public romancers like Nastassia Kinski, Oliver Reed; pontificators on the subject like Helen Gurley Brown, author of Sex and The Single Girl, Dr Alex Comfort, author of *The Joy of Sex*, Havelock Ellis, Germaine Greer; experimentalists like Byron, Woolf, Burroughs. Curiously enough, Aquarius is not a passionate sign; it's too mental and detached for that. Being an Air sign, it likes to keep life up in its head – so often sex is more in chat and in theory than actually lived out in practice.

At heart Aquarians are pioneers, explorers and anarchists. They like upsetting the status quo, or striding out into unknown territory, or discovering a new truth. Charles Darwin, whose theory of evolution certainly overturned the apple cart is in there, beside some fearsome feminists. All created controversy and forced society to rethink its beliefs. Explorers Freya Stark and Ernest Shackleton literally walked out into the unknown to show the way for more timid mortals.

Amongst the artists are wild, outlandish characters,

hugely talented but not easily restrained. Mozart's exploits were graphically portrayed in *Amadeus*. Bawdy, flagrantly unfaithful, he wanted to live life to the full by trying to have it all. His curiosity won out because society's good opinion meant little. Rabbie Burns and, in a different way, Lord Byron were not limited by convention. Byron, like Burroughs, experimented with life.

And Aquarius does produce a unique sense of humour, like Barry Humphries.

Aquarius in Essence

As a fixed Air sign, Aquarius often holds hugely stubborn views, but that is its strength. Aquarius doesn't care what tradition says, doesn't care what others want to hear, doesn't care if its beliefs are inconvenient – the truth is the only thing that matters.

Most of their passion is reserved for the truth. At a personal and emotional level, Aquarius likes to maintain distance. Most Aquarians like fairly free and open relationships, where both partners are tolerant of the other's need for space. It can be quite a claustrophobic sign if it feels jealousy and possessiveness lurking about in the atmosphere. 'Give me freedom to be myself' is their eternal cry. Anything that smells of manipulation, of an attempt to turn them into what they are not, or to coerce them into compromise, is regarded as the ultimate betrayal.

Down at the bottom line, most Aquarians would rather opt for any number of impersonal, fairly laid back friendships than one total, deep commitment. Passion is avoided because it traps and binds.

Although extremely experimental and very open-minded to anything modern, Aquarius can be irritatingly rigid in outlook. They just loathe being persuaded, cajoled, charmed or bullied into seeing other people's way of life, or way of thinking. 'What's that got to do with me?' they snort. 'I know I'm right'. Everyone else usually realizes they are right in two weeks, six months or five years' time, because Aquarians always know things ahead of their time. Sadly for them, by the time others have caught up to agree, they have moved on somewhere else. So the sense of being continuously misunderstood is always there. It normally adds a streak of irritability to their nature: constantly being out of step is uncomfortable.

Aquarius is one of the few signs with two rulers: Saturn and Uranus. Together they are the agents for change and innovation, but it does make the Aquarian temperament one which swings between the traditional and the radical. Part of Aquarians' constant tension comes from this conflict. They are an edgy wound-up sign, more so even than Gemini. Both are Air signs, and therefore not grounded in patient earth or soothing water, but Aquarius works at ten times the speed of Gemini. It has the high speed, electronic energy of a computer.

Aquarius and Uranus, indeed, rule computers, electronics, radio, TV, astrology and, curiously, archaeology. The ultimate truths, rooted in the past and ultra-modern high tech both fascinate Aquarians. But it is that computer-speed brain which often floors non-Aquarius. The conversation hops seemingly illogically all over the place, but it isn't illogical. It's just Aquarians' ability to flip through the reasoning processes at silicon chip speed, dispense with the topic and move on to virgin territory. Plodding brains get badly left behind, and generally reap the benefit of Aquarius's snappy tongue.

With a mind of this cast, inventiveness is high on the list of talents. Don't expect the Aquarian to actually make the invention – they aren't practical – but the idea behind it is no problem at all.

Essentially it is not a sporting, physical, natural sign. The joys of sploshing around in wellington boots, sweat, and being exposed to the elements, are not instantly attractive. Sitting, feet up, to watch it on TV is quite a different matter.

Friends are desperately important. Aquarians like lots of them, and generally won't give them up when they settle down with a partner. They tend to take part in group activities, and often work for humanitarian causes – the great brotherhood of man is important. Aquarians love humanity in all its forms, whatever its background or race.

Positive Traits
Independent, humanitarian, willing, friendly, progressive in outlook, original and inventive, are reforming spirits, faithful, loyal, idealistic, intellectual, noble, stimulating, effervescent, individualistic, courageous, curious, knowledgeable, active, ultramodern, have integrity.

Negative Traits
Unpredictable, eccentric, rebellious, contrary, tactless, stubborn, perverse, think the world owes them a living, unfaithful, isolated, impatient, anarchic, disrespectful, excessively bizarre, careless, intellectually arrogant, self-centred, asexual, and over-detached.

Aquarius' Winning Streak
Your intelligent inquiring mind, that pays no heed to the consensus view and will stick to its opinion against a huge weight of disapproval, is what moves civilization on. You need extremists to change society. A sweet, gentle hint doesn't revolutionize outlook; an abrasive, stubborn approach is what is needed.

Society would fall to bits if it was full of anarchic Aquarians, but equally, it will suffocate without that wonderfully rebellious spirit prodding it into enlightenment every so often. Aquarius carries the water of knowledge which the human race needs to keep developing to survive.

Capitalize on that wonderful tolerance you have: you understand that people can co-exist side by side, all living out their own individual lifestyles. You may not relate superbly well personally, since compromise is so difficult, but you give to others the ultimate in human dignity – the right to be themselves. You can extend the hand of friendship to almost anyone.

Aquarius as Lovers

Will have read all the right books, the most up-to-date, will know the theory better even than Virgo, but the practice is a bit more problematic. Aquarius isn't inherently a passionate sign, and doesn't really feel at home in the physical realm. Aquarians like variety, they like open and unconventional relationships, and they insist on a massive amount of freedom. They suit other Aquarians quite well.

Lovers have to be good friends as well. Like Sagittarians, they do like a good pal beside them in bed. They aren't necessarily very interested in sex, but if they are, they will be intriguingly experimental; just don't expect too much emotion with the fun. They absolutely insist on two things: a good level of communication, and not the faintest whiff of jealousy. But if you do strike up a compatibility, you will find an immensely loyal, faithful lover.

Aquarius Get On With

The other Air signs suit best, especially Gemini, which has the same restless curiosity. Other Aquarians often make a good match. Libra is a minor problem, since Libra likes to be approved of and Aquarius doesn't always square with that. Sagittarius is an excellent combination. It likes freedom and travel, is fun, usually bright and chatty, and adapts to Aquarius's more stubborn side. Aries is next on the list, though the spats could get electric, as sharp opinions clash.

Virgo, though a touch stick-in-the-mud and too worried about respectable appearances, can keep up a good background relationship. Leo is a little too stubborn, and isolated Aquarius is envious of Leo's ability to be constantly surrounded by an audience.

Taurus is far too immovable and physical to gel well; Capricorn is a plain disaster because it is the complete antithesis of all Aquarius's contempt for social opinion.

But the water signs give Aquarius most problems, especially the jealous, moody Cancer and Scorpio. It feels drowned, or cornered by an octopus when near that pair. So they avoid them. Pisces could well be from another planet – a different species altogether.

Aquarius as Children

Tiring, in a word, since they are prone to hyperactivity. They crave excitement and constant change, loathe routine, and run a mile from rules and regulations. Permissive education, they will tell you, was designed for them. It might be lovely in theory, but in practice it turns out anarchic adults whose lives are in permanent chaos. So a bit of discipline drummed in is a help.

But they do need more free space than most kids to do their own thing, and they need material to keep that endlessly inquiring, inventive mind busy. Buy them a computer as soon as possible. You will find they are real duds at what bores them, they couldn't raise a spark of interest in some things. But at others, they are genuine geniuses. Just find their special talent, and peace reigns – briefly.

But you do have a maverick on your hands, one who will not walk in the middle of the road, is bad at cooperation, and downright tactless when pushed. Aquarian honesty is almost as punishingly direct as Sagittarian.

Settle for the fact that junior is destined to be a troubleshooter, a pioneer or an explorer. They will challenge you to your limits, but they can be a highly stimulating, stretching energy to have around. You won't be bored.

Aquarius as Wives

They do like a lovely home, preferably colourful, light and sunny, preferably full of music. And they absolutely insist on having a kitchen stuffed full of the latest high-technology gadgets. Curiously for such a detached sign, Aquarius is fond of home surroundings, and is attracted to the idea of a successful partner, as long as he isn't there too much! They do need space, and freedom to be themselves and maintain separate interests. Not desperately domestic, they prefer to spend time talking to friends, reading or watching TV. They usually have a friendly relationship with children, and their own are always outstanding in some way.

Aquarius as Husbands

Much the same as above. They can be exceptionally loyal, and durable as long as they are given enough free rein. They are inherently honest and straightforward, and really don't like the notion of deceit. If they do decide to wander, they will probably do it permanently. Don't expect a practical handyman. He may disassemble the TV just to investigate, but anything non-electronic bores him rigid.

Aquarius as Bosses

Can be impatient, and will expect you to keep up with his/her computer-speed mind. Keep the tape recorder always to hand – you'll need it. But you will be well-provided with every latest gadget under the sun to help you work with more efficiency. The office will be ultra-modern. If you don't like VDU screens and do like the personal touch, you won't like Aquarius.

Don't expect acres of sympathy over illness, but you can expect all the help in the world if you are organizing a neighbourhood complaints group. You will be expected to support all the boss's favourite causes from Oxfam to anti-apartheid to Greenpeace. On the whole, one of the better bosses.

Aquarius as Slaves

As natural born rebels, Aquarius make pretty terrible underlings. They are always trying to rock the boat, explain how the authority figures have got it all wrong, and how *their* ideas are the only ones to make sense. If you force them into submission they behave erratically, and can be hugely disrespectful. If you really shut them up, you will find odd things happen to the electrical systems, and accidents occur. All that crackly energy of theirs just flies out into the atmosphere.

Favourite Saying

'But I told you that five years ago and you wouldn't listen.'

Aquarius and Money

They are far too head-in-the-clouds to be good with money. Too practical, too boring and they are far too fond of friends and good causes. Aquarians give money away! Usually they rely on partners to keep them straight where money is concerned. Their bright ideas can pay off, as long as someone else handles the business side.

Aquarius Towards the Millennium

The profound psychological changes which threatened at points to pull your life apart in the late 1980s and early 1990s will have settled completely by 1995. Heavy pressures caused you to question almost every aspect of your career and personal life. By the midpoint of the decade you should have found your true path in life, the vocation which will bring you real meaning and purpose. Uranus moving into Aquarius for seven years in 1995 will shake you back to life with a lively bang. Now you intend to compromise for no one, and the really rebellious side of you will emerge. Your friends will start to change as you search for more depth in your relationships. A sweeter, vaguer personality will begin to emerge after 1998. The great turning point comes in 1999 when you make radical decisions about yourself. This is your moment of destiny at the crossroads.

Ronald Reagan
6 February 1911

At first glance Ronald Reagan may not seem the typical Aquarian – he looks too much the traditionalist to fit the unconventional mould easily. But if you reflect how much determination it must have taken for him to do what no one had ever done before – move from Hollywood B movies to the White House . . . then the Aquarian individualistic, pioneering stamp becomes clearer.

His conservative politics and materialistic outlook come from a comfort-loving Taurean Moon and three planets in Capricorn. Capricorn is the sign of the arch-capitalist. With Mars, the planet of energy and determination here, he struggled long and hard, submerging emotional considerations and family interests to achieve his ambitions.

His sugary, seemingly easygoing image of good-natured bonhomie comes from Jupiter opposed to his Moon. It certainly gives him an exceptionally sweet tooth. But behind the image is a man for whom work has always taken precedence over fun with the family and children.

He has two T squares in his chart. One emphasizes his Sun, giving him leadership ability, but also the need to be centre of attention. The other T square emphasizes his Capricornian nature. It helped him as he struggled on the long path to the White House. His ambition was overwhelming; his aims very long term.

He needed social prominence to help him overcome his early feelings of inadequacy and self-doubt. He always appears on guard, highly reserved and he does indeed distrust intimacy. Forget that icing-sugar smile: he rules with a rod of iron. He has obviously picked a wife who fits his needs. Nancy Reagan is desperately Cancerian, attracted by his power and drive and ready to prop him up with her maternal instinct.

Yoko Ono
18 February 1933

A wonderfully Neptunian Aquarian, Yoko Ono was obviously destined to be mystical and unconventional. Her Aquarian Sun sits in the colourful fifth house of her chart. She needs to act her life out in a theatrical manner. With Venus also in Aquarius, she was attracted to the open approach to relationships. What she really preferred were impersonal friendships rather than anything too passionate or too committing. With Saturn also lying close to Venus she is laid back, sophisticated but underneath she is sensitive and quite lonely.

A happy-go-lucky Sagittarian Moon makes her footloose and fancy free, and gives her a boost of optimism. It also encourages her lofty ideals, though in a fairly impractical way. The Neptunian slant of her chart gives her a Piscean visionary outlook as well. She desperately wants to help humanity, but often her kindness in the past would have been abused. She tends to believe the best about people and when disappointed she will recover by withdrawing into her own world.

That Neptune emphasis, of course, led also to her artistic talents, as well as her more mystical inclinations. Her painting as well as her musical interests compensate for a never very settled emotional life. Ultimately, she will gain her emotional stability from a relationship with the public. She desperately needs to work actively in the arts, or supporting services, where she can feel needed.

In some more detached relationship with the general public, her emotions will be grounded. Three planets in Virgo give her all the hardworking, perfectionist, crusading energies needed to pursue some Neptunian cause of her choosing. Neptune is creative, spiritual, and peace-loving. It is attracted to gurus and in its turn attracts devotees of its own.

Barry Humphries
17 February 1934

Barry Humphries bounced into the world with all the verve, vigour and volume of Dame Edna in full flow. The Sun in Aquarius was exactly on the horizon when he arrived, which indicates a lustily strong constitution and an extremely bouncy personality. It also makes him a double Aquarian; indeed, he is a quadruple one, since Venus and Saturn were also lurking around the sunrise. But when the Sun and Ascendant share the same sign, the effect is a full frontal onslaught, in this case of Aquarian eccentricity. It stimulates, shocks, electrifies, amuses.

Adding to the zip is a highly excitable Aries Moon, giving him a volatile, emotional nature. His temper will suddenly flare up and just as suddenly die down. He will leap into action without stopping to think, and cannot bear having his freedom interfered with in any way. Had he not become Dame Edna, he would have needed to start a revolution somewhere to soak up all that excitable energy!

His well-publicized drinking patch in his younger days is the result of an aspect of Saturn to his Sun, which Richard Burton also had in his chart. Life seems so hard, so depressing that drink seemed an attractive escape route. Once the more depressive aspects are overcome, it does give the drive for a successful career, though relaxation never comes easily.

Happily, with Sun on the Ascendant, he has an amazingly strong physical constitution and can recover quickly from over-strain, though he will need periods of peace in seclusion away from his adoring fans. With Mars in Pisces he can be too open to difficult atmospheres.

The other intriguing aspect in his chart is a mix of Uranus, Jupiter and Pluto. It makes him one-track-minded, adventurous and extremely lucky. His career always has had, and will continue to have, lucky breaks which suddenly open new avenues of opportunity for him. Pluto pulls these planets together, creating an intensely determined individualist, who is also a loner. Happily, he has made a supreme virtue out of what could have been a destructive urge by living out on stage a flagrantly eccentric character.

CHAPTER 14

PROSPEROUS PISCES

IN A NUTSHELL
Dreamers and explorers – movies and music.

Film

Liz Taylor, Michael Caine, Sir John Mills, Daniel J. Travanti, Rex Harrison, Betty Hutton, Peter McEnery, Tom Courtenay, Lynn Redgrave, David Niven, Eleanor Bron, Sydney Poitier, Joanne Woodward, Lesley Ann Down, Peter Fonda, Samantha Eggar, Julie Walters, Jean Harlow, Jerry Lewis, Isabelle Huppert, Patrick Allen, Bruce Willis, William Hurt.

Film Directors

Bernardo Bertolucci, Luis Buñuel, David Puttnam.

Music

Liza Minnelli, Mickey Dolenz, Neil Sedaka, Paul Jones, Elaine Paige, Mary Wilson, Peter Skellern, Harry Belafonte, George Harrison, Shakin' Stevens, Roger Daltrey, Terence Trent d'Arby, Elkie Brooks, Fats Domino, Johnny Cash, Al Jarreau, Nat King Cole, Michel Legrand, Patti Boulaye, Nina Simone, Antoinette Sibley, Rudolph Nureyev, John Lill, Kiri Te Kanawa.

Sport

Niki Lauda, Peter Alliss, Ivan Lendl, Alain Prost, Barry McGuigan, Robin Knox Johnston, Michael Whitaker, Joe Bugner, David Broome, Naomi James.

Politics

Robert Mugabe, Senator Edward Kennedy, George Washington, Neville Chamberlain.

Royals

Prince Andrew, Lord Snowdon, Lady Rose Windsor, Prince Edward, Prince Albert of Monaco.

Writers

William Boyd, Douglas Adams, John Steinbeck, Sir Stephen Spender, Edward Albee, Anthony Burgess, Lawrence Durrell, Piers Paul Read, Tom Wolfe, Victor Hugo, Anaïs Nin, Elizabeth Barrett Browning, John Updike, Voltaire, Robert Altman, Ronald Searle.

Art

Michelangelo, Renoir, Rimski-Korsakov, Vivaldi, Ravel, Handel.

Business

Sir James Goldsmith, Rupert Murdoch.

Explorers

Ranulph Fiennes, David Livingstone, Amerigo Vespucci, Sir Richard Burton.

Star Gazers

Galileo, Copernicus, Yuri Gagarin, Patrick Moore.

Thinkers

Albert Einstein, Schopenhauer, Linus Pauling,

Alexander Graham Bell, Bobby Fischer, Rudolph Steiner, Assagioli, Edgar Cayce.

Infamous
Adolf Eichmann, Joseph Mengele

Pisces are the great dreamers of the world; and famous or infamous they all love music, most are fascinated by film. Thus some luminous names from the movie business appear: Liz Taylor, Michael Caine, David Niven. Many film business people have strongly aspected Neptune in their charts, which rules Pisces. Many Pisces are keen amateur photographers themselves – the image is the thing. Lord Snowdon and his protegé Prince Andrew capture their dreams in a still frame, while Buñuel and Bertolucci create great artistry on moving celluloid.

On the musical side the talent is exquisitely pure – Kiri Te Kanawa and Nina Simone, very different singers but both possessing uniquely magnificent musical instruments in their vocal cords. There is something almost awesome about the top range of Piscean talent. Consider Rudolph Nureyev – at his peak, unsurpassable. Michelangelo, Renoir . . . their talent lies beyond words.

Even when the dreams are scientific, not artistic, the superhuman quality remains. There is Albert Einstein, arguably the finest mind of the twentieth century; Galileo, Copernicus, similar giant I.Q.s of an earlier era, who pioneered modern astronomy. Patrick Moore, who has a similar interest in the stars, is Pisces.

Pisces make great explorers, whether of land, sea or outer space. Yuri Gagarin, the first man in outer space, was Pisces. Dame Naomi James sailed single-handed round the world, Ranulph Fiennes led the Transglobe Expedition round the world, following in a great explorers' tradition of David Livingstone, Sir Richard Burton, and Amerigo Vespucci, after whom the Atlantic landmass is named. Rupert Murdoch and Robert Mugabe are also dreamers – of a highly practical variety. They are what T.E. Lawrence called 'dreamers of the day'. He says in the *Seven Pillars of Wisdom*: 'dreamers of the day are dangerous men; for they may act with their dreams with open eyes to make it possible.' Sometimes it gives a quite disconnected feel to Pisces: so wrapped up in their dreams, they don't notice the people round about. At the extremely cold fish end of Pisces where beyond-human really has become inhuman, you get the Eichmann, Mengele temperament.

Pisces in Essence

The essence of Pisces is elusive, intangible, delicate, in misty focus. Neptune, which rules the sign of the double fishes, is deeply creative, highly spiritual, kind, compassionate, and idealistic. It also tends to get lost in daydreams, TV movies, and romantic fiction, and all that misty quality can turn to uncertainty, if not downright dishonesty at times.

Pisces does not like being pinned down. Try to get hold of a Piscean and have a straightforward, full-frontal confrontation and you'll see the problem. They duck and dive, dematerialize and evaporate before your very eyes in a puff of smoke.

Being down-to-earth, feet-on-the-ground and facing up to reality just is not their style. They need to float free, to use that supersensitive intuition, that delicate emotional impressionability, then they function at their best. Trying to make them see common sense is like trying to turn them into a clod of turf. What is beyond the reach of the five mundane senses is much more their scene.

Their intuition, their sixth sense, call it what you will, is often superb. They soak in the unspoken signals in the atmosphere. Often they appear to have phenomenal luck, but really it is sixth sense which just gets them to the right place at the right moment, saying the right thing to the right person. Luck, of course, is a Jupiterian preserve and Pisces has indeed got Jupiter as its co-ruler with Neptune.

They hate fights, hate hassle, quite often feel lethargic, and not up to the struggle of everyday life. That happens when they don't give their imagination and vision enough of an outlet. It turns Neptune negative and it undermines confidence, and energy.

That explains the huge gap between Piscean types. At one extreme there is the vague, uncertain, timid, impractical little fish and at the other Liz Taylor and Rupert Murdoch. Little fish and big fish. The big ones tend to be voracious, and have dreams that take over half the world. There is no limit to Pisces' imagination, which is why stars and outer space, transglobe travel, and mammoth enterprises fit happily into their scheme of things. But the crucial point for all Pisces, little and large is that dreams have to be turned into reality. Don't just keep them in your head as pleasant fantasies for whiling away the hours.

Pisces is also a highly orgiastic sign. It likes to dissolve in an experience greater than itself, something which can break through the barriers of reality. Not physical enough to be a deeply sexual animal, it often looks to drink or drugs for its mind-bending experiences. Pisces needs to escape from reality – which is why it adores the movies. You can sink into the fantasy there in the darkness of the cinema, enveloped totally by the wide screen. Or more self-destructively, you can try to get the bliss experience on a drug trip or through the bottom of a glass.

Pisces' sympathy with humanity comes from this ability to go beyond its own personal boundaries and merge with the other person. Taken too far, however, it can be a problem. Pisces feel so much for the world's suffering that they can get paralysed by their sense of pain. Their kindness makes them fair game for con merchants. But that only happens to weaker little fish, who would grow much stronger if they would let their anger out and assert themselves. Pisces usually have great ideas in business, can be amazingly stubborn, travel a great deal, eat a lot, get psychosomatic ailments, and attract more stable partners.

Positive Traits
Are sympathetic, compassionate, humble, sensitive, adaptable, impressionable, kind, intuitive, receptive, devoted, serene, romantic, idealistic, musical, artistic, very seductive, mysterious, imaginative, psychic, visionary, ethereal, mystical, sentimental, generous.

Negative Traits
Are vague, careless, secretive, easily confused, chaotic, unable to cope with practical running of their lives, weak-willed, indecisive, demanding, jealous, unreliable, deceptive, evasive, dishonest, shy, secret enemies, good at self-undoing, whining, self-pitying, melancholy, cowards, cold fish, cruel, angry.

Pisces' Winning Streak
Really the positive asset to capitalize on is your ability to dream, to have a vision of what you want your life to be like; your weak spot is making that stick. You need to live your dreams out in reality. Leaving them rattling round your head just cuts you off from life. You need to boost your confidence to the stage where you can begin to back your own judgement. Your intuition is

superb normally, but you rarely act on it. Give it a try.

Turn your hand to a creative hobby or allow your imagination more elbow room at work. All that creative energy turns very foggy if left unused. Stay with people: your sympathy and ability to give is of immense value to you as well as to them. Your distaste for imperfection makes you want sometimes to steer clear of humanity – perfect they are not. But you need to relate positively all the time. That way you stay in touch with reality; and help others to catch a glimpse of your inner vision.

Pisces as Lovers

Where the whole glorious subtle art of seduction is concerned, none is better than a full-blown Piscean. Seductive and eminently seducible, practised in all the nuances, nothing crude, nothing overt. Pisces is a past master of the craft. They attract by their very mysterious, unfathomable appearance.

Once the grand seduction is over, they go one of two ways. One is straight into an orgiastic routine full of aphrodisiacs, drink and the whole Bacchanalian approach. They want to go so far into the experience of it all that it feels like drowning. Or they go evasive – because really Pisces is not a physical animal at all, and doesn't feel happy in the body and the flesh. Pisces really loves perfect bliss, perfect goddesses and gods, and sadly they only come in the movies. Up the golden staircase into the clouds doesn't happen in real life. So Pisces ducks out, goes vague, drifts into their own private fantasies – life stays beautiful in there.

Pisces Get On With

Almost everybody. They are an adaptable sign, so will bend round most personalities. On the whole they prefer to avoid Aries, who is far too confrontational. But that apart, they have no strong dislikes. Curiously, they do get on well with their opposite sign Virgo who grounds them, and gives them a sense of stability. Curiously also, they like Libra. I say curiously because as a Water sign they should find Libra too detached, but a nice bright surface Libran leaves Pisces free to live happily in their head.

Liz Taylor's famed passion for Richard Burton was a Pisces/Scorpio match and, although extreme, does show the difficulties this combination faces. As Water signs they should get on – but really it is too strong, too deep for Pisces, and too out of control for Scorpio. Cancer equally is not a good match, too weak on the masculine side, and far too awesomely strong on the feminine. A male Cancer and Pisces woman would drift aimlessly; the reverse female Cancer would eat Pisces male for breakfast. Not good news.

The other two Earth signs, Taurus and Capricorn, are a good practical prop for Pisces' dreamier side, and Leo fits the bill because of its strength.

Pisces as Children

If your tiny Pisces is prone to sitting in corners staring vacantly into space, or tells lies constantly, then you know the unreality factor is too high. Channel their creative energies into painting pictures, modelling plasticine, writing poetry, or designing doll's clothes – anything that gets their dreams out of the inside of their heads into daylight. You'll find the difference is astonishing.

If they are a timid Pisces, boost their confidence. Make them understand that they need to listen to their own judgement and not be swayed by everyone they meet. Weak Pisces waft around like seaweed in a strong current; they have to get anchored in themselves. Do try also somehow to persuade them that perfection comes in movies and TV commercials, not in real life. Also persuade them, as they grow into teenagers, that drink and drugs are bad news as a way of getting to nirvana.

Pisces as Wives

Pisces women can be incredibly sweet, submissive souls or they can be raging tornadoes. Either way they like strong, stable husbands who can manage the practical affairs of life. They usually organize a home full of books, full of videos and certainly full of music. For an emotional sign, they can be quite detached and fidgety when it comes to close one-to-one relationships. 'Do I really want to commit myself to this imperfect person?' is what they are thinking. Not that you aren't as good as you possibly can be. If you are their spouse, your major drawback is that you are human.

So half the time you reckon they aren't with you at all – they are away on a quite private plane. They do like rich food so the cooking is likely to be lush. They are usually maternal with kids. Their main drawback is a tendency to be passive, or to wallow in self-pity.

Pisces as Husbands

Not dramatically different from the wives, but it has to be said that the male of the species are probably more deceptive than the female. Maybe not downright dishonest, just slippery. He doesn't like being pinned down – to anything! He may stray more in the spirit and the thought than in the flesh, but you will often have a nagging feeling that he has slipped the leash and is up to no good.

Won't be practically useful except at mending the stereo, which will always be the latest model and magnificently tuned. He does need a strong, capable wife to allow his imagination to roam freely, while she is running the boring bits – like everyday life!

Pisces as Bosses

Some hugely successful executives are Pisces. But you can bet they all have superbly efficient, practical secretaries keeping the paperwork and travel details in order. Curiously, minor Pisces bosses, not the mammothly top-notch ones, can be quite domineering. They are probably trying to exert an over-macho, compensatory authority over the minions. But it doesn't come from a feeling of inner security. On the whole Pisces are kind, tolerant, broad-minded bosses who give decent wages, think of your sickness benefits, and buy lovely Christmas presents . . . if you remind them! Their memories are a weak spot.

Pisces as Slaves

They can look incredibly timid little shrimps if cowed, so appear obedient. But if their confidence is too eroded they won't function at all, just sit in a corner and stare vacantly into space. If their melancholy cloud ever lifts they will secretly start to undermine your position. Not in any way you can spot or prevent – just subtly, slyly, and you will find the wet rot seeping into your foundations. So either way, not as useful as slaves as their appearance might suggest.

Favourite Saying

'I can't possibly do that.' 'But I don't know what to say.'

Pisces and Money

Curiously for such an impractical sign, they have excellent ideas about making the stuff. But they can spend horribly impulsively, and do rather expect partners to make substantial contributions to the coffers. As long as someone else is filling in the tax returns, paying the stamps and adding up the bank statements, Pisces can do very well around money.

Pisces Towards the Millennium

Your future, which looked like pure chaos as the 1990s opened, became more straightforward by 1993. Then the light dawns. Saturn in your own sign prunes, trims, slims down and cleans out. You arrive midway through the decade in sparkling form, though aware of continuing changes ahead. Finances may be tough going until the end of the decade as you learn to be more serious, less vague. But it is your career which is undergoing such a complete metamorphosis as Pluto moves into Sagittarius in 1995 to stay until well past the millennium. Now you must search and seek to find real meaning and purpose in your life's vocation. Earning money to eat is no longer enough. The Eclipses in 1997 and 1998 are pointing the way ahead forcibly. A great deal of the past will be swept away as you turn yourself inside out to learn the secrets which you need to know.

Prince Andrew
19 February 1960

Truly on the cusp, Prince Andrew was born a mere few minutes after the Sun moved from Aquarius into Pisces. But his interest in photography and the sea indicate his leaning towards the sign of the fishes and old father Neptune.

He does not have an easy chart. With Uranus just on the horizon in Leo when he was born, he likes to feel respected, whilst at the same time being free to do precisely what he pleases. Freedom of action without interference is what he needs. With Pluto opposing his Sun, he can be domineering. He expects others to do what he wants.

But underneath is a desperately vulnerable emotional man trying to get out. With Scorpio Moon, which is hidden and quite secretive, on the point of a Sun, Uranus, Pluto T square, his moods are incredibly complex and variable. Security is extremely important to him and he easily feels threatened. His relationship with his mother veers between closeness and a need to be independent. He sometimes feels she is too possessive.

Despite all his inner emotional tensions, he will, as he matures, become more and more popular with the masses. He is well suited to dealing with the public, and finds the emotional nourishment he gets from his popularity very rewarding.

He will put much work and dedication into serving the Navy, and ultimately the family firm. The tradition and heritage mean a great deal to him, as does his status. He needs the security of children, and all will bring him distinction.

His emotional life will never be easy, whatever he may do in the future. He rises to prominence around 1992, at the time there seems to be a major shift for all the royals. He will be higher profile at a public level through his thirties and forties.

Elizabeth Taylor
27 February 1932

Liz Taylor has an extremely watery, emotional chart. She must sometimes feel as if she is floating on a stormy sea in a rudderless raft, blown hither and thither by the currents. As if all that water were not enough, she has erratic, unpredictable, rapid change Venus Uranus in her house of marriage. No one relationship could last a lifetime with those explosive energies there.

Like Prince Andrew she has a Scorpio Moon, secretive and proud, on the point of a T square. Thus she has emotional problems in her personal life, but the ability to tune with public sympathy. She needs to feel needed by her fans.

With Moon squaring Mars she would have been well-advised to avoid alcohol altogether. She has a tendency to let all her aggression and volatility let rip when alcohol loosens her inhibitions. Often, Moon square Mars charts indicate a life in which physical disorders have an emotional root. And her Piscean Sun occupies a chart area which is also vulnerable healthwise. Sixth House Sun charts make health a major life's issue. She needed to take greater care of her physical system than others, not to abuse her body and allow herself more time to convalesce from illnesses. She has, of course, had an amazing medical record with multiple operations and chronic back problems. Had she lived a quieter lifestyle, she might have avoided much of it.

Curiously enough for someone with such a passionate public image, she lacks earth in her chart, suggesting a temperament that is not happy in the physical aspects of life. She adores the romance, the glamour, the glitter, but solid, down-to-earth commitment is not her style.

Born as she was in the midst of the Depression Years, she has the Saturn Pluto opposition in her chart squaring onto Uranus. None of those who carry these Gothic aspects on their charts have escaped tragedy in their lives. At whatever level, their lives have been full of dramatic, not to say melodramatic incident.

Kiri Te Kanawa
6 March 1944
The New Zealand-born opera singer, the world's leading soprano, was born under mystical, magical, musical Piscean stars. Not only her Sun but also Mercury, which rules her voice and way of communicating, are in Pisces. She can lift her audience up to the stars and out into the cosmos, but there is more effort in her singing than just born talent. She had a really tough upbringing which prepared her for the

rigours of an international career. A childhood in which there were highly strung, at times rather risky, influences around her has given her a liking for constant excitement and travel in her life.

She can be ruthless on herself and others when need be, if the job requires it. She loathes interference and will have no one telling her how to live her life. A rather hard-edged, at times explosive, quality takes away from an otherwise vague Pisces temperament.

If none of this comes across in her warm, seemingly easygoing manner, it is because of a powerfully placed Jupiter Moon Pluto conjunction. She appears as a strong, feminine woman who wants nothing more than to put her audience at their ease. Moon Jupiter together are sentimental, lazy and gloriously addicted to food. Add Pluto and you have created a super-mother image, but she can be controlling under her pleasant smiles.

Venus in opposition to this conjunction adds, if anything, to the sugary charms which she can switch on at will for her audiences. She has a powerfully attractive personality which can create seductive magic out of a look, but underneath she can be a turmoil of emotions. Jealousy is a problem in her life, but she copes by staying fairly unemotional. With an Air Grand Trine she is able to rise above difficult feelings to chat unconcernedly about a great many subjects. Her mind is acutely active, though it can make her a little too detached at times.

With no earth in her chart, she is curiously impractical and ungrounded, often not doing enough to keep her body in trim. But it is her beautifully aspected Neptune which gives her those wonderfully tuned notes. Her great singing skills were God-given, but she has worked exceptionally hard to turn them into a long running and highly successful career.

CHAPTER 15

CHART SIMILARITIES

Sun sign astrology is relatively simple, slotting personalities into one of twelve signs depending on birth dates. But when you add information about the time and place of birth, a much more complex picture emerges, and throws light on the profound intricacies of the human mind and spirit.

Carl Jung, the father of modern psychotherapy, once said that a birth chart could take two years off the beginning of an analysis, because it produced such detailed information about the personality. It lays out talents, traits, hang-ups and patterns with minute precision.

Those who share similar birth charts, known in the trade as astrological 'twins', are relatively easy to find if they share the same date of birth. Their life patterns tend to be very similar, though the energies often play themselves out in different ways. I share, for instance, an exactly matched chart with an opera singer and a near fit with a British Cabinet Minister. I have neither a voice nor political ambitions, and they certainly keep their paranormal interests well hidden, but the drives are the same, the career and emotional ups and downs remarkably similar.

By chance I stumbled across one almost exact replica

between Prince Charles and Martin Luther, the quite theatrically intemperate German founder of modern Protestantism in the sixteenth century, who was condemned as a heretic. Prince Charles's 'monstrous carbuncle' speech, which caused such a stir, is but a pale shadow of Luther's scourges of the Catholic Church. His highly personal attacks were fuelled by his Scorpio intensity, and his firm belief that he had a mission to deliver the truth.

Evangelism lives on in Prince Charles, though he has had to find alternatives to the Church as a focus for his crusading energies. Establishment medicine and modern architecture have taken the brunt of his spiritual beliefs and public pronouncements. He may not have nailed them to a door as Luther did in Wittenberg, but his architect protagonists obviously wince under the onslaught just as much as the Vatican did four centuries ago. Both share a curious drive to reform while still upholding the status quo. They look backwards and forwards at the same time.

Luther was deeply pessimistic and superstitious, believing firmly in demon possession. Prince Charles' often sad demeanour certainly mirrors this trait, while his oft-spoken-about dabblings in the paranormal certainly indicate a belief in something out there.

All that furious Scorpio drive and dogged determination drove Luther to write one book a fortnight at one point in his career – a total of a 100 by the time he died, at the goodly age for those days of 63. So the Royal publishing industry can take heart.

Luther started his life as an Augustinian monk, though he later married a nun and extolled the virtues of family life. That central spiritual drive is equally obvious in Prince Charles and the other two Scorpios with fairly similar configurations at birth – Billy Graham and St Augustine. The celibate ascetic always fights a battle inside Scorpio with an equally strong human need to indulge. The spirit and the flesh need to come to a compromise with each other.

Since the saints congregate together, it is no surprise to find the sinners doing likewise. The Marquis de Sade, with his hard porn fantasies, shares an astrological pigeon-hole with the English murderer Neville Heath, the Yorkshire Ripper Peter Sutcliffe, and the 'evil monk' Rasputin who controlled the Tsar's family in Russia through his paranormal powers.

All were Geminis with explosive Mars, Uranus, Neptune patterns at birth, creating an attraction for dangerous situations and a pathological dislike of interference. They had the Gemini split personality – one side normal, sociable, bright, the other side dark, brooding, depressed. Rasputin is not primarily known for his murderous tendencies, but he certainly died a spectacular death at the hands of assassins. His amazing powers kept him alive after repeated attempts to shoot, bludgeon and drown him.

My historical researches through the dusty astrological charts of the past two thousand years turned up fascinating, though not unexpected, connections between Queen Elizabeth II, an unflinching Taurus, and Catherine de Medici, the dominant 16th century Queen of France, who exercised power through her sons. Though Eva Perón, the Argentinian upstart, also shares in this formidable Taurean drive for control, which rather takes the aristocratic shine off.

More intriguing are the links between Piscean Prince Andrew and Sir Richard Burton, the Victorian explorer and translator of erotica such as the *Kama Sutra*, the *Perfumed Garden* and *Arabian Nights*. Burton's personal researches into the sexual practices of exotic natives were a constant trial to his long-suffering wife, Isabel, who was always left 'to pack the bags and follow on behind'. She took her revenge after his death by burning all his diaries, which must have been a treasure trove of gynaecological idiosyncrasies. Both men share a Piscean Sun closely aspected by Pluto and Uranus, producing a domineering temperament which demands total freedom.

Both share a highly passionate Venus Mars contact. Prince Andrew's falls in earthy, sensual Capricorn, though his tendency to wander is firmly held in place by a highly conventional Saturn in Capricorn which no doubt reminds him of the dignity of his position. The Duchess of York was obviously less patient, less submissive to the whims of men than her Victorian predecessor.

The Princess of Wales at nineteen looked like everyone's ideal daughter-in-law – sweet, demure, helpful. She has developed into a woman of sophistication and undoubted determination which can only strengthen with the years. She is a stalwart Cancer, the sign of matriarchs from Rose Kennedy, mother of the famous clan, to Barbara Cartland, novelist extraordinaire. The appearance is usually sympathetic, even sugary, but the core is solid steel.

The future Queen's chart bears striking resemblances to that other Cancerian powerhouse, Nancy Reagan. One of Cancer's great failings as a mother is the need to produce perfect works of art as children, which in Nancy Reagan's case has led to an almost complete breakdown of relationships in adult life, but the ex-First Lady is more controlling than her British counterpart.

Diana is strong-headed, argumentative and dogmatic because of a combination of Mars and Pluto, but that aggressive streak is multiplied several times over in Nancy Reagan's chart, which reeks of hostile antagonism. Nancy wanted power without opposition, and would use whatever means were available to get it. When her public reputation sagged, she turned to charity work against drugs to revive her motherly image, but that has been dropped recently.

Both Cancerians are chock-a-block with initiative, drive and energy, but with Jupiter Saturn contacts strongly in their charts, their destiny will always tend to be at the mercy of larger social issues. Disappointments over a long period of time can drag Jupiter Saturn personalities down. Both are prone to hefty mood swings and major downers.

Another American ex-First Lady, Jackie Onassis, intriguingly has more than a few connecting links to Princess Anne. Both are impulsive, headstrong Leos, who are fanatically keen to protect their brood from the dangers of the outside world. Both are constantly in the public eye, constantly on the move, and find it difficult to relate in great depth because of a sense of inner insecurity. Leo always gives the impression of self-confidence, but the aura is more often than not a hollow shell. Inside there is a sense of nothing, of not really existing as an individual. Work is their way of validating their existence and creating, however temporarily, a sense of self-esteem. Both had rather cold mothers but supportive grandparents. Princess Anne is the more high-handed and dominating of the pair, and her drive to be a public figure of influence and repute is quite intense.

Back in the realms of world politics, Mikhail Gorbachev stands shoulder to shoulder with his astrological twin – George Washington, the political father of the United States and symbol of national independence. Both are visionary Pisces, but their charts have an underlying toughness and ruthlessness. The horrors of the world and the ways of men hold little that is strange for them.

Pisces are day dreamers and fantasists, often deeply creative but just as often out of touch with reality. Washington and Gorbachev, however, are of that breed to which T.E. Lawrence refers in the *Seven Pillars of Wisdom*: 'All men dream: but not equally. Those who dream by night in the dusty recesses of their minds wake in the day to find that it was vanity: but the dreamers of the day are dangerous men, for they may act their dream with open eyes to make it possible.'

Washington, two centuries before, shared Gorbachev's great dream of freedom and independence. He was a man of patience, courage, indomitable will-power and formidable personality, who fought through to victory in the War of Independence. At times he was hanging on by his finger nails. In one memorable winter, after resounding failures on the battlefield brought on mainly by the disloyalty and disorganization of his own troops, who often deserted him, he retired to Valley Forge to lick his wounds, considering surrender. But his strength of will held out and he met the spring with a hardened, more efficient army and rode to victory.

Cliff-hanging crises seem to bring out the best in both men. They share an unrelenting quality from a rather unlovable but highly useful Saturn Pluto Jupiter configuration in their charts. They are loners, laws unto to themselves and not too concerned with the social niceties of life if it gets in the way of progress. Gorbachev, it is true, is more of a revolutionary reformer, tends to head for the explosive change and was always in danger of sudden downfall. Washington has a slightly mellower feel. But both had the ability to tread a difficult middle ground in their domestic politics.

Less obvious is the astrological match for our greatest politician of this century, Winston Churchill: Steven Spielberg, Hollywood film director and billionaire. High-flying, excruciatingly optimistic Sagittarius is the sign of Churchill and Spielberg. They have Moon Saturn Pluto influences, indicating a childhood of particular unhappiness. Since Sagittarius always looks for the silver lining, they both escaped into fantasy. Spielberg has often said that his films, like *E.T.*, were really made for the child in himself. Churchill created an inner fantasy land of great heroism and lived it out in politics. Both have depressive's charts; both use it as a spur for their achievements. Churchill referred to his 'black dog' which always followed him around. At Britain's moment of deepest gloom in the war he could rouse the nation to courage, because he had so often had to do it for himself. His imagination and faith were what pulled the nation round. Spielberg's movies have a recurrent theme of suffering overcome, as in *The Color Purple* or *Empire of the Sun*.

Both have known great hostility to themselves despite their best efforts, which is a rerun of their childhoods where nothing they ever did was enough to please either parent. Both, with strong Uranus influences to their suns, are rebellious mavericks, are not scared to walk down unknown paths. Both are loners who do not know how to relax and mix with the crowd.

A fascinating sidelight to Churchill is that, like Adolf Hitler, he has Neptune and Pluto in an area of the chart which suggests an almost occult use of power and influence. Churchill had precisely the same power as Hitler had to lift the collective psyche and mould it to his wishes. Both could tune into mass feelings.

Astrology often indicates this linking between great enemies as if their destiny lay together in some strange way. Fate may seem as if it makes strange bedfellows, but psychologically speaking, opposites are often as close together as those who appear the same.

CHAPTER 16

PRINCE CHARLES/ PRINCE WILLIAM

Will Prince Charles ever become King of Britain? Or will his eldest son Prince William succeed Queen Elizabeth in his place? Those are questions which astrologers have been asking now for some years. Prince William, it is argued, has a traditional regal chart where Charles has not. Undeniably, William will be on the throne by his thirtieth birthday, perhaps even by his mid-twenties around 2006 AD, when Charles is only in his late fifties, and the Queen, if she survives like her long-lived mother, will be 80.

So what does Charles' chart show of his destiny and the next twenty years? The layout of planets at his birth indicate an introvert, a mystic, a great originator of ideas, but one who also wishes to serve the masses. With a fourth house Scorpio Sun, he needs to delve deeply inside to find himself. What he achieves in the outer world is less important than what he accomplishes in terms of soul growth and inner development. As was discussed in the previous chapter, he is intriguingly similar astrologically in certain major respects to Martin Luther.

The argument about a fourth house sun is that home and the interior life are more important than career, and therefore success and prominence are less likely, but well known figures like David Bowie, Rupert Murdoch, the Emperor Hirohito, Albert Schweitzer, Proust and Herman Melville were also born when the Sun was at its lowest point in the heavens.

With the North Node of the Moon in his 10th house of career, his reclusive tendencies will vie with his need to develop some sense of his own authority, and usefulness in his career. In this respect he is less well-designed for the rigours of the monarchy, which demands absolute dedication, commitment and single-mindedness. A fourth house Sun usually has a strong drive to distinguish a personal identity separate from the family background. His leanings toward Jungian psychology, with its strong bias towards individuation and the need to break away from suffocating family bonds, is part of this quest.

He suffers because his father could be said to lack a real masculine role in life, as reflected in the fourth house Neptune. Jung defines the masculine as being able to set goals and knowing how to get there; neither Philip nor Charles carry enough of this energy. It resides too much with the Queen, the Queen Mother and Princess Anne. Anne indeed is better suited, astrologically speaking, for the conventional monarch's existence than her brother is.

Other classic signs which mark out Charles as the Puer Aeternus, the psychological name for the creative boyish spirit which finds difficulty in growing up to accept responsibility and commitment, are the Mars Jupiter conjunction in Sagittarius in the sporting fifth house opposing explosive, rebellious, breakaway Uranus. Charles' dangerous, at times irresponsible sporting exploits spring from here. He needs too much adventure, stimulation, excitement and travel. Routine, discipline, dedication and commitment – the stuff of the Queen's existence – are anathema to him. He fears the claustrophobic involvement of too close a one-to-one relationship.

Does this mean he will never attain the throne, does not indeed wish to? Not necessarily. His 10th house Moon gives him a need to serve to the public's needs from a position of prominence; he wants recognition. Many politicians have this placing. He is sensitive to public mood and has the potential to sway mass feelings. His Moon close to the north node, as it is in Mother Teresa's chart, reflects his need to 'mother' through his career, to cater for other's needs, feeding and housing them. Hence his desire to see the dilapidated inner cities brought back to life.

He is also, I suspect, trapped in his position. The fourth house Neptune is common amongst those who are born into 'enmeshed' or 'bound' families where sacrifice is always demanded on behalf of the family. Also, his strongly emphasized first house Pluto in aspect to both Sun and Moon suggests that he feels powerless to resist the family pressures, however hard he struggles to break free to establish an identity for himself.

That Pluto indicates how frightening an experience he found life when he emerged from the womb. It occurs frequently in the charts of babies born by Caesarean. Deep inside, they fear for their very survival, and death seems more likely than life. For ever after through life they put up a shield of defensiveness against the world and other people to keep away threatening influences. This need to protect privacy is also found in the charts of Greta Garbo and Marlon Brando.

Charles' life has not been easy, and will not be in the future. He has difficult lessons to learn, and many internal negativities to clear out. He has difficulty stopping himself running vendettas against those who have hurt him, as he sees it. But the heartening aspects of his fourth house Sun and the Taurus north node are that the end of his life will be peaceful, harmonious, contented. His great love of the earth, of gardening, and of nature will ultimately repair a breach in his relationship to the feminine. He will no longer fear commitment and involvement.

His moment of reckoning was always destined to be in the early 1990s, especially 1992. An astrologer at his birth would have predicted heavy psychological pressures as the old structures of his life were torn down. Massive changes would be unavoidable in his personal life and relationships to his family. Unpredictable and sudden upheavals would also have been seen in the British chart around the monarchy in 1993. Similar influences to those which have accompanied changes of the monarch in the past are present at this point. In career terms Charles becomes higher profile through the 1990s from 1992 onwards at the point where the Queen takes a much less active part in public life, probably due to health worries. Princess Anne and Prince Andrew also move centre stage in the early 1990s. The peak of Charles' public career comes when he is 49, in 1997, lasting to 2006 when he is 58. He could be on the throne then. A very unhappy mood surrounds Charles in 2006 when Prince William moves forward to pick up the reins of office.

Interestingly, Princess Diana is more evident in the spotlight during William's reign than she appears to be beforehand. She may wield the mother's grip on the British throne which has become a tradition in recent years. William's chart, with its strong emphasis on Cancer, is likely to make him a mother's boy. A New Moon suggests a personality who has less need to relate on a one-to-one basis than most, and this is coupled with a seventh house north node which certainly indicates delay or difficulty in marriage. But, paradoxically, the Sun and Moon in the seventh stress his need for the security of a partner in all his dealings. He may well cope with this contradiction by sticking closely to his mother, publicly and privately.

Jupiter at the midheaven of William's chart marks him out for a life of power, brilliance and leadership. He wants to be noticed, and will seek fulfilment through his career. Pluto close by adds determination and will-power to his high energy and enthusiasm. He will be a law unto himself, but capable of exerting the full majesty of his office.

Saturn and Mars in Libra, on the focal point of a T square relating to Sun, Moon and Neptune, will force him to learn to stand a life of military discipline and suit him for executive position. However, he will be domineering, explosively bad-tempered at times, resent interference and is liable to burn himself out with over-activity. His opinions, like his mother's, will always be strongly felt and forcefully delivered.

Underneath the strong will and warlike tendencies, he worries endlessly, to the point of paranoia, and is not well grounded. But the Cancerian new Moon in the 7th is a sure sign of a public personality. He thrives on the glamour, romance and image of his position. In some ways, his main relationship in life next to his mother will be with the public. Although moody, he projects his personality well.

With a largely upper hemisphere chart he sees life in outer, objective terms, whereas Charles' lower hemisphere suggest a much more subjective approach to life.

William moves out of the wings into a higher profile position when he is 18, and moves further into the spotlight when he is 22. Saturn has now moved above his descendant heading for the midheaven, which it reaches when he is 30. This is normally a career high period. His grandmother, Queen Elizabeth, was crowned as Saturn moved through her ninth house. Mrs Thatcher became Prime Minister as Saturn hit the midheaven.

So by the age of 30, he should be firmly installed as King William. What of Charles? Since the birth chart never indicates death, there is no way of knowing whether he will be around to see his eldest son crowned, but the indications are that the end of his life is content. After 2006, when William rises in public prominence, Charles sinks into the background. Although the initial years may be difficult, Charles would revel in the time and inner space his seclusion brings for his spiritual life. Ultimately this is his search and salvation, much more than the pomp, glitter and outer pageantry of a monarchical existence.

CHAPTER 17

ANATOMY OF A ROYAL MARRIAGE – THE DUKE AND DUCHESS OF YORK

The breakup of the marriage of the Duke and Duchess of York, while sad, was almost inevitable. Their relationship chart was fraught with tensions from the beginning and underwent a series of phenomenally trying influences from the early stages onwards. Were it not a Royal marriage it could have broken up three years earlier. In easier times it might just have survived, though it would have required a great deal of mutual effort in private, perhaps with counselling to resolve the psychological problems between them. But a shaky relationship stuck in the goldfish bowl of Royal public life in the 1980s and 1990s stood no real chance of patching itself together.

For two such uncompromising individualists marriage was never going to be easy, despite public declarations of happiness, and its evidence in passionate kisses in the full glare of the world's press.

Neither was brought up in a harmonious family background. Fergie, like the Princess of Wales, saw her parents' marriage split. She remained with her father, a man whom she idealizes. Andrew saw his parents, though remaining together, as highly incompatible. Thus neither have a good role model to follow. Indeed, the tradition of royal marriages has been of a well-polished public unity and an often catastrophic private reality.

Prince Andrew, surprisingly, is the more emotional of the pair. Born just into Pisces, he also has a highly emphasized watery Scorpio Moon. His needs for security are paramount and he is constantly seeking a mother. He was the Queen's favourite child, and it is no coincidence that several years into the marriage the couple were still living in Buckingham Palace. Letting go of his childhood dependencies and his past has not been easy for him.

His touchiness, oversensitivity and moodiness make personal relationships an area of conflict. He desperately needs an ideal, very stable home base. His mothering instincts are probably stronger than the Duchess of York's and I would suspect it was his driving force that encouraged her to undergo pregnancies against her inclinations, and produce children about whom she is obviously highly ambivalent.

With strong Sun Pluto influences in his chart, reflecting his experience of a domineering, rather manipulative father, he can be incredibly demanding and unreasonable, but with an equally strong Uranus on the ascendant, he also demands total freedom for himself: a case of 'you do what I want and I do what I want'. He is not an easy man to live with in harmony.

Humility is in fairly short supply in his character, and he can stand on his dignity a touch too much at times. His royal status is important to him, which is where his reputation for arrogance in the navy comes from. Reputation and status are all-important to him, but this very conventional outlook must have taken badly to his wife's public gaffes. When she once tripped coming out of a nightclub while heavily pregnant, he froze; her detective picked her up. Those are not the reflex reactions of a Falklands helicopter pilot who must be instantly alert; those are the horrified reactions of a proud man who loathes public embarrassment. Yet he has picked a wife whose energies are constantly running out of control.

The combination of Scorpio Moon and Venus, Mars and Saturn in Capricorn also make him highly defensive and secretive about his true feelings. He can appear cold and rather cruel, but in truth he is terrified of being hurt so he puts up fairly impenetrable barriers, even to those closest to him. Sadly, he lacks a sense of humour which could have been a saving grace over the rougher patches. His greatest emotional nourishment will come in his middle years from his public work, at which he will be surprisingly popular and successful. Somehow his emotions sense safety in numbers, and an adoring public at a distance is easier to handle than a close relationship which brings up his fear of being suffocated, possessed and invaded. His calming, protective side will emerge towards his forties. As a father he will be benign and enthusiastic. He is genuinely happy around children, and his own will bring him great good fortune.

But long-range commitment to a close relationship will always be extremely difficult for him. With Aquarius on the cusp of his house of relationships, he craves a totally open marriage where he can wander at will. He will need a very long rein indeed. This is something his father appears to have been given, but the Duchess of York was not bred to have the Queen's overwhelming sense of public duty and the need to keep private rifts out of sight.

Like Charles, he very evidently lacks a strong male model from his father who, in marrying the Queen, completely submerged his own individual needs to her rank and way of life. Like Charles, Andrew tries to bolster his sense of masculinity by bravado, but deep down in the core of himself he feels unable to assert his masculinity. He is the son of a matriarchal household, and he must free himself from those fears of being dominated. If he cannot, he will increasingly need to fly to freedom to assert himself.

The Duchess of York, as a Libra woman, tends to be more 'masculine' and outspoken by instinct, and like Mrs Thatcher, another Libran, she has Mars close to her Sun giving her a particularly fiery, hard driving, argumentative temperament. Her boisterous approach and obsessive interest in sport derive from this over-identification with her sporting father.

Her early mothering experience was not good, with a sense of a powerful but cold mother who did not provide a sense of stability. Her own racketing around during the first pregnancy with Princess Beatrice, and her abandonment to follow Prince Andrew for twelve weeks just after the baby's birth echo her own sense of her early days. Her damaged relationship to her mother prevented her integrating a healthy attitude to the feminine. The young Princess's own chart shows a mother who is rejecting, erratic, highly tense and unstable. Beatrice's own adult emotional relationships will follow in the same family pattern as the Duchess of York's and her mother's.

The Duchess very much fears being over-controlled and pushed around by women and her own emotions. Her relationship with the Queen, however equable it seemed on the surface, was fraught with those tense fears. The Royal courtiers who tried to curb her lifestyle must have put her into rages. She resents any interference in her plans, as was quite obvious from the controversy about her going against Royal tradition to keep the larger part of the royalties from her Budgie books. Despite the resignation of her private secretary and the public outcry, she pursued her own course.

With her highly excitable Aries Moon in square to chilly Saturn, she learned to clamp her own emotions down early on and, like Andrew, can appear ruthlessly cold about family and emotional matters. But underneath there is a highly vulnerable, lonely, undernourished child. She will tend to attract herself in life to men who undervalue her femininity, indeed are scared of it, as she is herself. At this level she could be like Mrs Thatcher and the Queen, the kind of woman who sacrifices emotional relationships for the sake of status, work and duty. But her personality is more complex and her life more challenging than that. A close Venus Pluto contact pulls her in quite the opposite direction. Her passions are very strong. Obsessive sexual passion is common with this influence. It produces a temperament which is intense, proud, often achingly loyal, but has an unfortunate tendency to attract itself to relationships where betrayal is all too common. That, perhaps, also gives a hint of why she left her baby so long to be at the side of her husband, whom she feared would stray.

It is a *sine qua non* of relationships that they can only work as well as the two individuals who make them up. If they find their own emotions hard to handle within themselves, then no partnership on earth can paper over the cracks. Neither were handed a happy legacy in emotional terms by their parents, and it was too hard for them to forge a marriage that went beyond their own childhood experiences.

What was supportive about their relationship chart was a supremely strong Jupiter, which generally brings health, wealth and good fortune, and can mitigate, or at least cover over, deeper insoluble problems. They did communicate easily at one level, confidently, though very noisily. Ego conflicts raged as both stuck grimly to their opinions.

Home life was exceptionally important to both, though both opted for a slightly formal, rather chilly place where work took precedence over pleasure. Money was and is highly important to both – neither could be happy as normal struggling young marrieds. Both are supremely status-conscious and dependent on the expensive luxuries of life to boost their sense of self-importance. They had sporting interests and zany friends in common. But their relationship needed a strong interaction with the outside world to survive. Andrew's long absences away on naval tours of duty were perhaps one of the main killers of the relationship.

Their relationship did bring to the surface, even more than usual in marriage, previously hidden psychological characteristics. They needed to deal immediately with whatever came up: anything left to smoulder ultimately came through with such fiery intensity that the relationship was irrevocably damaged. In some curious way their highly unconscious interaction with each other had a strong effect on the world around them, and this in turn attracted hostility, even enmity.

Prince Andrew is undoubtedly becoming higher profile through the 1990s, more successful, possibly coming more into the public limelight. The Duchess herself may feel pushed into a corner and resentful. She will not really emerge to take up a stable life until the mid 1990s, by which time many of her inner psychological problems will have eased. He faces a tremendous emotional upheaval, deeply affecting his relationship to his mother and his family through 1993 and 1994. Only after that will life begin to offer the hope of harmony.

Marjorie Orr
YOUR OWN PERSONALISED HOROSCOPE

Computer calculated to fit your exact time, date and place of birth.

1. YOUR TWELVE MONTHS AHEAD in detail. What the stars hold in store for you in the coming year.
£12.50 Please tick ....❑

2. YOUR BIRTH CHART – an in depth analysis of your potential, temperament, talent and blockages.
£12.50 Please tick ....❑

3. FRIENDS & LOVERS – the key to that strongest relationship in your life.
£12.50 Please tick ....❑

Full name to appear on report ....
Address to be sent to ....
....
....

Male ❑   Female ❑
Date of Birth: Day ....Month ....Year ....
Exact Time of Birth..
Place of Birth ....(nearest large town)
City/County .... Country ....
Daytime Tel. No. ....

FOR FRIENDS & LOVERS REPORT: *Please state partner's details*

Full name to appear on report...
Male ❑   Female ❑
Date of Birth: Day ....Month ....Year ....
Exact Time of Birth..
Place of Birth ....(nearest large town)
City/County .... Country ....

Cheques / Postal Orders made payable to:
STAR QUALITY PERSONAL HOROSCOPE OFFER
& send to: P.O. Box 1357, Shepton Mallet, BA4 5ED